MEAN PEOPLE SUCK

How empathy leads to bigger profits and a better life

MARKETING
INSIDER
PUBLICATIONS

Marketing Insider Publishing,
div. of Marketing Insider Group, LLC
1069 Country Club Rd
West Chester, PA 19382

978-0-9970508-3-7 Paperback
978-0-9970508-4-4 Audiobook
978-0-9970508-2-0 Ebook

Ordering Information:
Special discounts are available on quantity purchases by corporations, associations, and others. For details, contact michael@marketinginsidergroup.com.

 CONTENTS

To all my previous bosses, customers, and colleagues...the good, the bad, the insane...I am truly grateful.

And to my current bosses: my wife, Liz, and children, Sophie, Ava, James, and Luke. I am truly lucky.

MEAN PEOPLE SUCK

How empathy leads to
bigger profits and a better life

MICHAEL BRENNER

"The mass of men lead lives of quiet desperation."
~ Henry David Thoreau in *Walden*

Introduction

I've held numerous jobs throughout my career. One day, I sat down to count them all. I knew there were many, but the number turned out to be higher than I thought. When I was done with my final tally, I counted 53 jobs.

My working life started in 1983 when I was 12 years old. I had just made my middle school basketball team. Back then, everyone wore the 1983 Dr. J Converse All-Stars. They were white leather high tops, and I didn't want to be the only one on the team wearing old sneakers.

I asked my parents if they would buy me new shoes, but I was the third of fourth child and we didn't have much money. My dad worked in a factory, and my mom stayed home to take care of the kids. They couldn't buy me the shoes, but they told me that if I wanted them so badly, I could get a job. That's how I became a paperboy. I delivered newspapers at 5:00 a.m. every day and I got those shiny new sneakers.

Later in my teens, I worked at a concession stand at our neighborhood pool. I also stocked shelves, worked the checkout line at the local grocery store, counted night deposits in a vault at my local bank, and spent a summer scanning over tiny rolls of microfiche film to look for scratches in old bank records.

The shortest job I've ever had was when I worked at a pizza place for four hours. They put me in the broom closet with a chair and a little TV and told me to watch a four-hour instructional video. I thought they were kidding, but I watched the entire video inside that little room in the dark. I am mildly claustrophobic, and it felt mean to stick new employees in a closet for four hours. So, I walked out and quit.

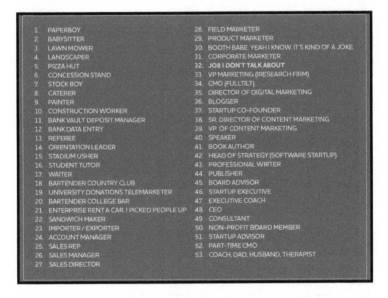

1.	PAPERBOY	28.	FIELD MARKETER
2.	BABYSITTER	29.	PRODUCT MARKETER
3.	LAWN MOWER	30.	BOOTH BABE. YEAH I KNOW. IT'S KIND OF A JOKE.
4.	LANDSCAPER	31.	CORPORATE MARKETER
5.	PIZZA HUT	32.	JOB I DON'T TALK ABOUT
6.	CONCESSION STAND	33.	VP MARKETING (IRESEARCH FIRM)
7.	STOCK BOY	34.	CMO (FULLTILT)
8.	CATERER	35.	DIRECTOR OF DIGITAL MARKETING
9.	PAINTER	36.	BLOGGER
10.	CONSTRUCTION WORKER	37.	STARTUP CO-FOUNDER
11.	BANK VAULT DEPOSIT MANAGER	38.	SR. DIRECTOR OF CONTENT MARKETING
12.	BANK DATA ENTRY	39.	VP OF CONTENT MARKETING
13.	REFEREE	40.	SPEAKER
14.	ORIENTATION LEADER	41.	BOOK AUTHOR
15.	STADIUM USHER	42.	HEAD OF STRATEGY (SOFTWARE STARTUP)
16.	STUDENT TUTOR	43.	PROFESSIONAL WRITER
17.	WAITER	44.	PUBLISHER
18.	BARTENDER COUNTRY CLUB	45.	BOARD ADVISOR
19.	UNIVERSITY DONATIONS TELEMARKETER	46.	STARTUP EXECUTIVE
20.	BARTENDER COLLEGE BAR	47.	EXECUTIVE COACH
21.	ENTERPRISE RENT A CAR. I PICKED PEOPLE UP	48.	CEO
22.	SANDWICH MAKER	49.	CONSULTANT
23.	IMPORTER / EXPORTER	50.	NON-PROFIT BOARD MEMBER
24.	ACCOUNT MANAGER	51.	STARTUP ADVISOR
25.	SALES REP	52.	PART-TIME CMO
26.	SALES MANAGER	53.	COACH, DAD, HUSBAND, THERAPIST
27.	SALES DIRECTOR		

In college, I worked mostly customer service jobs, such as a rental car agent. These kinds of jobs taught me how much mean people suck.

After I graduated from college, I first worked in sales for almost 10 years in various roles, selling to both retailers and manufacturers. After that, I moved into marketing. I took a short-term job that I don't like to talk about, became a CMO with a couple of different companies, ran digital and marketing teams for a software firm, then started speaking and writing. Eventually, I started my own company.

While working 53 jobs for 25 years inside corporate organizations and start-ups alike, I've witnessed unique management styles, workplace cultures, and bosses, all of which taught me a few lessons about business and how to manage it all. I've learned that sometimes your boss sucks. Sometimes your customers suck. Sometimes you just want to get your job done without being challenged or questioned. But the real question is...

How happy are we in our jobs? Most people I talk to are unhappy with either their jobs, their bosses, their employers, or their career paths. I often hear about the challenges that so many of us face right now. I've seen how a business environment can impact individual job satisfaction, career aspirations, and workplace culture. So many of us feel stuck; we feel like the victims of decisions over which we have little control.

The data backs this up. Gallup, who surveys the attitudes and behaviors of employees, customers, students, and citizens all over the world, has been researching job satisfaction for decades. In their latest polling[i], Gallup found that 34 percent of us report being engaged in our jobs, 53 percent of us are disengaged, while 13 percent are actively disengaged. I'm not sure what "actively disengaged" means, but I assume those are the employees sneaking away with office supplies and calling in sick every chance they get. They don't want to be there and only show up to work to collect a paycheck.

It's hard to look at those statistics and not wonder about their impact on low morale. Morale affects how we feel as humans, the way we treat others, the overall success of businesses, the economies these businesses drive, and the governments for which we vote. So, how did we get to this place of low morale?

To answer that question, we each need to look at our own work experiences. We need to decide which category we fit. Are we happy in our current roles, or are we actively disengaged? Have we always known what our passions are? Do we love our bosses, our companies' cultures, or our current paths?

Like most of us, I've had jobs that I've loved and others that I haven't. Not everything was perfect about those positions I cherished and not everything was awful about the jobs with which I struggled. So, what separates the positive experiences from the negative? In other words, what makes us either love or hate the work we do? What makes us love or hate the lives we live?

After working so many different jobs and speaking to thousands of people at conferences all over the world, I learned that most of us want to do jobs that we enjoy and that make some impact on our companies. We want to make a difference with the talents we enjoy using but something tends to get in the way. What is it? The overwhelming answer I've heard comes down to one thing: we think mean people suck.

We know they're all around us, but we don't know what to do about it. We feel stuck, victimized, and even brutalized. Many of us feel alone, and we suffer silently. It starts by ruining our day. Then, before we know it, we act out toward others, inflicting some of that pain and frustration on those around us.

One of the first things we humans learn to do is mimic our parents. Our first lesson in life is to act like others so that we can understand them. We call this empathy, and it's the ability to understand and share the feelings of another.

To illustrate empathy, have you seen the video of a young girl who cries during a dinosaur movie[ii]? In the most adorable way, the girl is sad because the dinosaur she is watching gets hurt. She knows what it's like to fall and get hurt, so she tells him to get up and find his mommy because that's what she would do.

We learn early on to feel sadness when other people get hurt. We learn in school about the golden rule to treat others the way we want to be treated. We learn that bullying other kids is not nice. We learn the Ten Commandments. We meet firefighters, police officers, and people in the armed services and learn that service to our communities is a good thing. We know that we should be kind and have empathy, **but why do so many of us, especially in the business world, not display empathy for others?** As we get older, what causes us to lose empathy?

Cambridge researcher Dr. Varun Warrier studied empathy[iii] and found that, unlike the fight-or-flight reflex, we are not born with empathy. It is a learned trait; we develop empathy over the course of our lives. He also learned that women have a higher propensity toward empathy.

In the *Journal of Patient Experience,*[iv] Dr. Helen Riess talked about a series of studies that shows how medical students tend to have less empathy for patients with each passing year of medical school and residency. This happens despite these students being taught that empathy improves the patient experience and leads to faster recovery times.

The University of Michigan Institute for Social Research[v] found that we are 40 percent less likely to describe ourselves as having empathy for others today than we were 40 years ago, with the steepest declines coming in the last 10 years. Looking into the impact of this declining empathy on our political systems, Professor David Sparkman found[vi] that our self-reported empathy and our perception of others correlates to the political party with which we affiliate. Finally, the State of Workplace Empathy Study[vii] found that 92 percent of CEOs think their companies have organizational empathy, while less than half of employees agree.

Although we are born with the capacity for empathy and we learn to value empathy throughout most of our childhood, something happens as we get older. I call this the paradox of confidence. We think that shrewd and self-confident people are the best ones to lead. However, overconfidence often correlates with insecurity, and arrogance is often a mask for deep-seated self-doubt. So, who is a better leader: The arrogant or the humble? Who is more likely to fight for employees and customers?

If you think of all the bosses you've had over the years, how many of them have been genuinely nice people who treated you with respect and showed you empathy? I'm sure there were some. I've been lucky to have had a few. Being kind isn't yet a lost art but those managers can be few and far between. It's counterintuitive to what so many of us think we need to do to get what we want.

But why does it seem like this is a much bigger problem in today's world? Why do people seem to suck more? Why do our bosses seem to suck more? Why do politicians seem to suck more? What has changed? Well, a lot has changed over the past 25 years. We live in a world that has been radically disrupted. It may be easy to think that change doesn't have much of an impact on us but unfortunately it does.

When we start by looking at the way we communicate with each other today, we see that we are all connected. We have more ways to communicate than ever before. But as connected as we all are, basic human interaction takes a backseat and empathy has become a crucial variable that often gets overlooked or dismissed.

Technology and social media have led to more impersonal forms of communication that make it much easier for us to be mean to each other. Our significant others can dump us over text. Our bosses can fire us over email. People shoot down our ideas on Twitter, kids get bullied every day on Instagram and Snapchat, and negative comments flood platforms such as YouTube. Today, we can anonymously spew so much hate without any real fear of repercussion. That wasn't the case 25 years ago because the technology didn't exist. It's become the norm. We're used to it and we almost expect it because, frankly, the digital world has made it easier for people to be mean to each other.

Unfortunately, this disconnect and lack of empathy has permeated into business. In today's fast-paced, hectic office environments, who has the time to worry about how the person sitting next to us feels? Despite my own good intentions, I've been guilty of this myself. I'm sure that most of us can think of a time when we have decided to put ourselves ahead of someone else because we were tired, stressed, or just didn't care.

It makes sense that sometimes we need to put our own needs ahead of others to fight for what we need and want. But imagine the world if all we did was try to dominate others. We need empathy for the world, our families, our communities, and our businesses to fully function. And what we may not always realize is that empathy is the counterintuitive secret to getting more of what we want.

Today, too many businesses, and the people who run them, don't recognize that **infusing empathy into our workplace cultures also makes for a more profitable and stable business model.**

The State of Workplace Empathy Study finds that 42 percent of CEOs recognize the need to display more empathy but they don't know where to start.

If we expect our employees to spend so much of their time at work, we should make it worth their while. Employees will be happier for it and they'll be more invested in the work they do. We all do better work when we care about our jobs.

The lack of empathy that managers have for employees, and that people have for each other, is a significant problem that impacts business success and life satisfaction, but it's only half the problem. It's too easy to point the finger at someone or something else. It took me a while to learn what the other half of the problem is, even though it was right under my nose the entire time. And looking back, I guess it should have been obvious.

More than 10 years ago, I was hired by one of the world's largest enterprise software companies as their first head of digital marketing in North America. I had no budget, so they wanted me to assess our current activities, see what was working and what wasn't, and find ways the company could optimize a budget.

I ran a couple of reports and looked at all of our marketing campaigns, which were supposed to drive new business leads for our sales organization. Then I ranked them from best to worst. What I found shocked me: A large percentage of our marketing campaigns had delivered zero leads and added zero value to the company. I expected to see some campaigns do better than others. But knowing we had spent millions of dollars on them and seeing that more than half of our marketing campaigns were completely ineffective, it almost looked like it was on purpose.

I was so shocked by the data that I think I even used the word "criminal" when I described it to my new boss. I knew we were wasting money but I didn't know why. I also knew from my dozens of previous jobs that if we focused our marketing efforts on helping our customers, then we should be able to show better business results. I had to fight hard to get my boss to approve this more empathetic approach, but I was finally given a few months to test my theory. After all, I couldn't do worse than what had been done before.

So, I gathered the budgets from those campaigns into one centralized marketing program that focused on delivering the content that our customers wanted. As a result, we saw millions of dollars of revenue flow into the company. In fact, for every dollar we spent, we gained $18 in revenue. This was the most successful program I had ever managed, and yet, the foundation of it was simple: empathy for our customers delivered results for the company.

The marketing people who had wasted so much money were the ones who ultimately got much of the credit with our sales teams. They looked like rock stars. But why had that simple notion of empathy eluded them? What drove them to waste all that money? The data was available to everyone, so why didn't they use it?

That was an eye-opening moment for me. My colleagues were very smart people. Surely, they wanted to do the right things and make a positive impact but so many of them didn't. Why didn't they? And how could so many smart people, with truly good intentions, be so epically wrong?

To help answer these questions, I looked back on my previous jobs and recalled similar frustrations. That realization set me on this path to figure out why we are so miserable much of the time. Why do we suck? Why is it so hard to have empathy for others and to just be kind?

The closer I looked, the more I realized that this was not just a problem in marketing. Most of us spend much of our time at work trying to please our bosses. We don't want to get fired. Self-preservation kicks in and we largely do what we're told. This explains why my colleagues were wasting budgets and not even looking at the results of their campaigns. For them, success meant doing what they were asked to do, whether or not it was good for the company and whether or not it delivered results.

So many of us spend our time trying to please our managers and trying to be good corporate citizens. But it is exactly that behavior of self-preservation (some would call it "butt-kissing") that causes us to do things that may not work. That's when I realized empathy was the missing piece of the puzzle. We must actually care—care about our customers, our managers, our employers, and our fellow employees. Something has to break the cycle of blindly doing what we're told by our companies or managers.

If we could turn it around, even for a second, what would we see? I believe that if companies valued empathy, even stated it publicly and documented it as a core value, we could start to turn the tide. If companies were to treat employees with a little more respect and if managers gave employees a little more room to serve customers' needs, then we could create better, more positive experiences for customers. Those customers would spend more money with our companies and stay longer. Then our companies would grow and hire more happy employees, and the virtuous cycle could begin again.

I know that the word "empathy" and the advice of "be kinder or nicer" can sound trite in our cynical world. And I realize how naïve it can sound that if we follow the golden rule and treat others the way we want to be treated, then others will return the favor.

But as a consultant, a keynote speaker, and someone who has had 53 jobs, I have found that this message is the foundation of my success. I therefore try to teach the importance of empathy to the clients and audiences whom I feel honored to address.

Some might call empathy by other names like customer experience, employee engagement, or patient experience. Many companies talk about the bigger problem without addressing the underlying cultural problem they need to fix in order to achieve business growth. The cultural problem is that employees and customers want a company and managers who care about them. They want improved customer experiences, they want to feel valued by their bosses and employers, and they want to feel cared for when they go to a hospital.

When we improve those experiences, it directly translates into the increased revenue that every CEO so desperately desires. But telling a CEO that he or she needs more empathy may not go well. I've tried. I once told a room full of CMOs that building a culture of empathy was their number one job, and one of the CMOs remarked to me that she had too many things to do to make culture important.

Building empathy isn't just about marketing and it's certainly not the job of human resources to fix culture. Building a culture of empathy is about us and how we feel and perform at work. Leaders who create a more desirable work environment while treating their employees with respect will see the kind of growth that they want to achieve.

Far too many business leaders these days believe that going the extra mile for customers and employees is a waste of time in an age when younger workers can change jobs at the drop of a hat or when the economy is in a downturn. That instinct couldn't be further from the truth because, as we're beginning to see, empathy is the counterintuitive secret to success in business and life. It starts with us and extends to our jobs, our employers, and our colleagues.

We're all customers, and as customers we ultimately want to support brands and businesses that share our values and who care about their employees, the environment, and their impact. Many companies say that they want to put the customer first but it's amazing how few companies actually do.

To illustrate this, think about a current example of a company that has made mistakes repeatedly. There might be plenty that come to your mind. For me, it's a bank I've used for years and despite their claims of caring about their customers, we hear news about how this company lied, deceived customers out of their money, and pressured them into opening accounts they didn't want. We also hear about how it all started with pressure from the top of the organization to focus on growth over people. We can conclude that this company has a culture problem!

Empathy may be something of a business buzzword, but I'd argue that it's still underused given how little of it we have in our current culture. To me, the word is often misinterpreted in the business world, and it is too often forgotten in everyday life. There are plenty of leaders who think that empathy is soft and subjective. Some may believe that "Empathy is for losers! Winners focus on getting the job done." Other leaders might think that it's the job of human resources to build a solid company culture, but there is very little HR can do when employees despise their work environment.

Through a culture of empathy, we can push back against the

status quo and the work environments that makes us feel disconnected. Developing a culture of empathy isn't some hippie, new-age notion of employees feeling better at work. It's about all of us finding meaning in the everyday tasks we perform. It's about attaching ourselves to a vision of something bigger. And it's about delivering real innovation and impact that we can be proud of. Isn't that something that every business leader and working professional wants to accomplish?

I know it's not easy. It's hard to resist our natural tendency to focus on what we want and concentrate instead on what we can do for others. Creating a culture of empathy requires a lot more effort, but it's worth it because good things happen to those individuals and companies who do.

Some readers may not believe this or may still be skeptical, but I want to show how you can get what you want with empathy. I'll share stories, examples, mental frameworks of companies, and what I call champions—individuals who have used empathy, made other people more important, and achieved success beyond their wildest dreams.

The bottom line of this book: *empathy for others is the key to getting the lives and careers we want.*

If you are unhappy in your career, you have the power to change your situation and make a massive impact on your life and in your businesses.

We are all experts in something with passions and talents that we want to share with the world. As humans, we have a tremendous capacity for empathy. The pressures of life today make it all too easy to forget about what others want, but that's why we find ourselves lost and further away from our goals.

We can transform our lives, our work environments, and even our entire company culture into something better, no matter where we sit in the org chart. I know it may sound like I'm taking on a relatively large agenda, so I'm honored that readers are willing to take this journey with me. I hope that readers get at least one thing from this book that can help and maybe be shared with others: **mean people suck, and life's too short to be miserable!**

Chapter 1:
YOUR JOB SUCKS

"It just isn't working out."

I tried to get more out of my boss during that impromptu Friday afternoon meeting in his office, but he just kept repeating that same line. I was fired, and it couldn't have come at a worse time. Not that there is ever a good time to get fired but my wife, Liz, and I had just moved from Chicago back to the Philadelphia suburbs so we could raise our first child where we both grew up. We were staying with Liz's parents while our brand new house was being built.

After that meeting with my boss, I left the office and drove to an empty parking lot nearby. I sat there, flip phone in hand, trying to muster up the courage to call my wife and break the news. I didn't know what to say because I wasn't yet able to wrap my head around it. How did this happen?

Three months earlier, I was on top of the world. I was 30 years old and had just landed my dream job as the head of marketing for a medium-sized company on the outskirts of Philadelphia. I was going to be a leader—the VP of the marketing department.

My first job was to come up with a solid marketing strategy to fix the communication problems we had with customers. I was told to increase brand awareness, generate leads for the sales team, and develop new messaging. It was a significant amount of responsibility for one person but I didn't care. I was thrilled to finally be able to work with such autonomy and have the permission to get creative. Or so I thought.

My first instinct was to fix the perception we had among existing customers and the potential customers we were already talking to. Who spent more time on the ground talking with our customers than the sales team? So, that's where I started. They were all open and happy to share their frustrations; I got the sense that no one had ever asked them what was wrong with the company's marketing. We got off on a great foot, and they put me in touch with some of our customers so I could pick their brains as well.

I then went to speak with some of the other departments to get their feedback. I saw gaps that needed to be filled, and I put together a plan to revamp our strategy to help the company, and specifically our sales team, better connect with the market.

Before I went to my boss, I wanted to test the waters. I ordered a dozen pizzas and brought in the sales team and other employees throughout the company to listen to my plan. I wanted to gauge their reactions and so was pleased that the feedback was positive. I rode a wave of confidence when I set up a meeting to present the feedback to my boss, the company president.

The meeting with my boss was less encouraging. As I presented the strategy, the air in his office hung heavy. There was no enthusiasm, only the lingering smoke from his two-pack-a-day habit. I could tell that he wasn't really listening at all, but I pushed through anyway.

I respectfully explained why we needed to change and laid out the approach we had to take if we wanted to grow. I even showed him pictures of some of the customers I talked with and wrote fancy quotes above their heads. Then, I delivered the closing line that I had practiced over and over, "With your approval, I can get started right away, and with minimal investment, I believe we can start seeing revenue increases within a few months." BAM! I nailed it!

I looked at him with wide expectant eyes as he stared at the document that I had spent so much time preparing. Finally, he pushed it back to me and delivered the bad news. He told me that 10 years earlier, he had become company president because he had cold-called "the phone book" and that had led to lots of sales for the company. He had been given huge sales commissions and, he explained, he didn't need any of this "marketing."

He explained further that, although he had hired me to run marketing, the company was seeing a decline in sales. So, not only would the company not implement my suggestions, he felt instead that my time would be better spent cold-calling potential customers along with the sales team. He stood up, grabbed his pack of cigarettes, and left the room. Wait! What?

My ego took a hit, but I was no quitter. I took a deep breath and decided that I had to make it work. For the next six weeks, I sat at my desk calling potential customers and pitching our services.

There might be nothing harder in the world of business than cold-calling unsuspecting people. During one semester in college, one of my 53 jobs was calling alumni and asking for donations. It didn't go well back in 1991 and it certainly wasn't any easier in 2004.

Because I had started my career a decade earlier in sales, I thought I could make it work. It had to, for my new family if nothing else. But what I realized the hard way, at least for me, was that any success I had had in the past was all about building relationships, not about calling cold prospects who had never heard of me or my company.

Despite putting forth my best efforts, I was not cut out for the task. After 20-30 calls a day, week after week, I made a grand total of one $12,000 sale. I guess I shouldn't have been surprised when I was called into my boss' office that Friday afternoon and fired. It felt like a waste of time, but I did learn that my boss didn't care about me. He pretended to care about me, but he cared more about the company's bottom line. By pointing me into a role in which I had no chance of being successful, he created a situation where everyone lost. Mean managers suck! This manager was the worst boss I have ever had, but fortunately that isn't the end of the story.

WHAT'S THE BIGGEST CHALLENGE?

Whenever I give a speech to business leaders in marketing, sales, HR, and customer teams, I ask the audience, "What's your biggest challenge?"

Today, no matter where I'm speaking, the answer is the same: "Our biggest challenge is showing some kind of business results and impact—something like increased sales or a return on investment." For these business leaders, it is no longer about hiring ad agencies, it is now about a return on investment (ROI).

I find that every functional role in every business is starting to experience that same pressure, especially during our dreaded annual performance reviews. (Seriously, how are these still a thing? Our boss sets up one meeting a year to tell us how we're doing? More on that later.)

What's causing this increased pressure to deliver measurable results? Technology, data, artificial intelligence, and new analysis technologies are allowing our companies and our managers to measure more things, predict future trends, and manage more resources. All the while, we keep getting asked to do more.

MEAN BOSSES SUCK!

For many of the marketers that I talk to, the situation looks something like this:

Your CEO comes up with an objective for the next couple of months to boost the return on investment of your marketing plan by 20 percent. As it stands, most of your marketing campaigns include targeted ads on established websites and social media platforms. Your team also creates a lot of promotional materials, such as sales brochures that no one reads, pens and stress balls with logos on them, and customer videos that have an average number of two views.

As a brilliant marketer, you see there's space in the budget for what we call content marketing. You create two to four blog articles per week that answer the common questions from your buyers. You know that this approach is the most effective way to attract new customers in the current business climate. You also think it would be great to combine this with some in-person events. It's a common tactic in the industry and you've seen the data. Getting people to associate your business with content that helps them and with events they enjoy attending will most successfully direct people to your company without smacking them in the face with the same promotional crap other businesses use.

You calculate that your company could create this content for just a few thousand dollars a month and you host an event for a few thousand dollars more. You know this is an effective way to acquaint potential customers with your brand without spending too much money. It's also all highly measurable. You can see what works and what doesn't and adjust the plan to increase ROI.

Potential customers will be more likely to do business with your company if they regularly engage with it in their social lives. Or, perhaps they'll just enjoy the content or the event and spread the word to other potential customers. Overall, it's a solid plan to spend a little money to yield a higher return. More importantly, you are confident that an investment in content and event marketing would boost the ROI right where your CEO wants it.

You sit down to discuss the idea with your CEO, but before you even reach the end of your pitch, he waves it off. It turns out he just got back from an event where he heard about a case study from a cool, hip consumer brand doing great stuff on Instagram. The CEO tells the CMO to start posting on Instagram because he heard that it's the future of marketing and he wants to get in on it before everyone else, "It's the 21st Century. We should get on Instagram!"

The CMO agrees that she's been waiting eagerly to get on Instagram, so she immediately puts pressure on marketing to start posting on Instagram.

In your head, you fight back, arguing that the last time you tried the hottest new social media trend, it didn't do a damn thing for your marketing ROI. But, she's the boss. So, you go along with that idea instead of your own. You figure out how to post on Instagram because that is what marketers do today.

Three weeks later, the CEO checks on the progress being made on Instagram but notices that your posts aren't getting nearly the number of heart "likes" he expected. He sends an email with a lot of exclamation points to the CMO, who sends an email to you with even more exclamation points, putting pressure on you to do "something." What do you do? You end up having to buy ads because that's also what marketers do today.

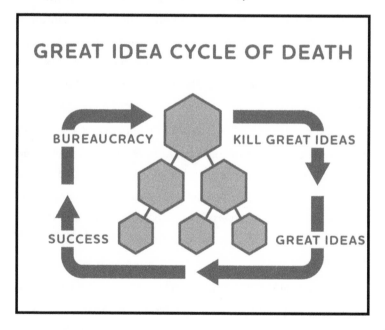

Three weeks later, the CMO returns from a conference where she heard of a great case study about Snapchat and how Snapchat can be great for a brand like yours. The CMO knows it can work and has a plan to sponsor rainbow puke Snapchat filters with your logo on them. You could push back, but at that point, it's too late.

You're already on the hamster wheel and the cycle is just beginning.

No matter our role in the company, this likely sounds familiar. This is true for the sales team, HR, and many other functions, as much as it is for marketers.

THE GREAT IDEA CYCLE OF DEATH

Plenty of the bad managers shown in these examples exist out there. We know the type. They assume they know what will have the most impact and what's most important without consulting other team members. They can't just tell us the objective and get out of the way. They insist we accomplish their goals their way. They're convinced they know what's best, even if they haven't the slightest clue how that aspect of business works on the ground.

Who suffers? We employees do. We must deliver the results but we're also being told how to do it. Companies may be competing to hire the smartest people but what good does that do if companies don't listen to those people? They treat their employees like followers rather than experts with experience and ideas of their own. Inevitably, we find ourselves frustrated and thinking, I told them so.

This is part of the "Great Idea Cycle of Death." We know we've done great work and had great ideas and some of those ideas worked to produce better results. Yet we don't get promoted, we don't gain more autonomy, because this is what happens to our ideas instead:

• Our great ideas produce some success.

• That success creates more bureaucracy, and our bad managers take all the credit.

- That increased level of bureaucracy kills great ideas.

- We get assigned to more projects where other people tell us what to do.

- The business results are not great, and we are miserable.

To illustrate this, we can refer again to the time I was fired from my marketing job:

- Excited to make an impact, I gathered incredible insights from our executives, sales team, and customers on how to improve our marketing approach (great ideas).

- I shared with them my marketing plan and my goals of improving our brand awareness and getting more leads and revenue (success). They all thought it sounded great!

- But I needed the company president's approval (bureaucracy).

- He killed my ideas.

- He then insisted that I start cold-calling, which didn't work.

- I got fired.

I'm not saying that we shouldn't have to get our manager's approval for some things, especially when budgets are involved. But I do think companies need to trust in the smart people they hire to get the job done. And companies need to try and cut bureaucracy wherever they can to allow for employees' great ideas to become successes.

THE ILLUSION POINT

One of the challenges that we marketers encounter specifically is that most people who watch commercials think they are marketing experts and fully understand marketing. They know a good ad when they see one, right? That belief gets amplified by a thousand with CEOs, some of whom rose up through the corporate ranks long before the social web, mobile technology, and hashtags (#FTW!) even existed. Combine a reluctance to change with the ego we see in so many CEOs and it is no surprise they convince themselves that they are experts, even if the data doesn't support their ideas.

THE ILLUSION POINT

TIME
MONEY
HARD WORK
SACRIFICE

DISENGAGED EMPLOYEES
FRUSTRATION
FAILURE
LOST OPPORTUNITY

The point at which our managers switch from fielding input on a goal to directing us into counterproductive tasks is what I've dubbed the "Illusion Point:"

- The company president asked me to make sales by cold-calling companies (the tip of iceberg).
- I spent every day for weeks trying to make that work.
- I wasted my time and the company's money.

- I could have been adding real value instead.

- I failed.

- He was frustrated.

- I got fired.

Many managers don't only want to assign a big-picture goal, they also want to have a hand in the execution of each step along the way. Often, the steps they have in mind for reaching the goal are counterproductive. The goal then doesn't get accomplished and the cycle restarts itself.

Succumbing to the Illusion Point is so frustrating for those of us who rarely see our good ideas make it past the first meeting. It also costs our companies money and wastes our time. Still, it's hard to combat the Illusion Point. I can understand that most of us want to avoid risking our reputations with our bosses to fight battles we're unlikely to win.

WASTED EFFORTS

I was relatively successful when I started out as a salesperson— only one other person sold more than I did in the whole company. I attributed that success to focusing on my clients. When I went to clients and just tried to sell them stuff, it didn't work very well for me. But when I sat back and listened to them, when I asked real questions because I was genuinely curious about them and their business—when I showed them real empathy—I started making sales. Who knew? (I also had some amazing managers who let me figure that out on my own!)

In the end, I thought I could help more of our customers as a marketer, working to create the solutions to our customers' biggest problems. So, when one of those roles became available, I made the switch from sales to marketing.

In that role, I learned we had a problem. Our sales team sold our customer data to manufacturers, detailing where and how their products sold. A separate sales team sold a different set of data to retailers. So, after speaking to both the manufacturers and the retailers, we agreed that it would be a better idea to build one centralized online platform that used the same data but sold to both parties. Today we call this "the cloud," but back in 1998, it was a new concept.

After prototyping and validating the idea with customers and the sales team, we started working on the global rollout. It was going to be a big deal for our company and one of the biggest technology investments they had ever made.

Our team had been working with an agency for six months to prepare a direct mail campaign to tell all our customers about the rollout of our new idea. We came up with more clever ideas and spent a lot of time and money testing those ideas. For example, we chose red packaging because that's what testing had shown to have more impact and we wanted it to pop out at people! Right before we were about to launch, the CEO approached us and said he preferred the packaging to be blue and not red. The company logo was blue and he didn't like red.

In the end, the campaign launch was delayed for weeks and tens of thousands of dollars were spent changing the packaging from red to blue, even though testing showed red to be the better option. I couldn't believe we had spent so much extra money and wasted so much time because of the CEO's subjective whim.

I recognize that I actually liked the CEO. He had earned his position. He deserved my respect, and I gave it to him. But that was the first time I can recall starting to think that there had to be a better way. I know that I felt like I was letting myself down. I was chasing the whim of the CEO so that he could be happy, but I was wasting time and money working on a small detail that would undoubtedly hurt our results.

According to consulting firm SiriusDecisions[viii], 60-70 percent of the content that companies create is completely ineffective. This is an important stat. It may include content that gets created but never published or possibly content that gets published on an unseen web page five layers down from the company home page. It may even include content that gets created and then left behind or forgotten about. These scenarios happen every day inside companies.

This statistic is worth repeating. I think it's important that we understand the potential of what companies could do instead with all the money they spend on content that is 60-70 percent ineffective. Research has identified this as close to a one hundred billion dollar problem[ix] just for business-to-business organizations.

To explore this, I gathered data from more than a dozen business-to-business companies with whom I've worked. I looked specifically at those that ran marketing campaigns where the goal was to generate some kind of measurable business result, such as an email address, a lead, or actual sales revenue. What I found was that more than 50 percent of those campaigns didn't produce anything even remotely measurable for their organizations.

The simple fact is that there is a lot of wasted effort out there and it is not confined to marketing. Too few leaders even bother to notice. They just go home every night hoping that their team listens to them and does what they are told.

While most company CFOs and COOs likely don't miss an opportunity to remind us to keep costs down and give constant updates on the ROI, we have to ask, "Why do we do all this stuff, even though we know it won't work?" I have found that it is because:

Behind every bad idea is an executive who asked for it.

The best way to stop wasted efforts, to break through the Illusion Point, and to start adding value or delivering more ROI is:

We must start by saying no to requests we know won't work.

Not being able to say no was the reason my colleagues ran marketing activities that didn't work, not even a little bit. They were smart and they knew better, but a manager had asked them to do it and they had felt powerless to push back.

While I have empathy for anyone in this situation, it's a cop out. It's easy to pass the buck and blame the CEO, the CFO, the executives, sales teams, our boss, all the bad managers, and the product experts who ask us to "do stuff." It's easy for us to say they all suck and don't know what they're talking about, but we are the ones who still do all the stuff that doesn't work, aren't we?

On a personal level, we know we need to put some kind of value over blindly doing what we're asked to do. You may have learned the 80/20 rule, also known as the "Pareto Principle" that suggests that 20 percent of our efforts will account for 80 percent of our results. I think we're all subconsciously assessing what that 20 percent of highly effective activities is. So, why do we still do the tasks that maybe we even know won't work? Why do we stay on the hamster wheel?

Often, we're so desperate to please our bosses that we say yes to every request we get. We hope that doing all of this requested "stuff" will translate into something good for us, when deep down inside we know that it won't. We then become resentful and start to question ourselves. We wonder how our career got off track. This is the Illusion Point.

While this chapter is about how mean managers suck, my first call to action is to employees: Stop doing more stuff! If we want to love our jobs and have real impact, we can no longer keep doing stuff that won't work just because we're asked to.

Admittedly this is easier to say than it is to do in real life. I hear too often from employees that their bosses are jerks or that their companies are very "old school" and traditional. They don't feel ready to push back.

It may help employees to recognize that it's not always the boss' fault and that he or she has his or her own issues and bosses. The first step is to find common ground and then find a way to look good to the leaders above you.

You can have a cake, but you can't tell me how to bake it!

I once had a boss who seemed grumpy all the time. I assume that he had learned from all his previous bosses that it's best to act like a tough guy. He would hold status meetings that felt more like he was holding court and asking his minions to come forward and beg for mercy. He would give employees lots of tasks. I learned later that he was actually a nice guy, a loving dad, and a good person. It just didn't feel like it at the time—when our entire team would meet and discuss ways to cope with the boss' ridiculous requests.

Because I was the newest member of that team, the boss asked me continually to do stuff that I didn't think would work. I eventually hit my breaking point, and instead of saying yes, I asked him how I could help him. I asked him what he wanted and needed. When he explained it to me, I told him that he couldn't have his cake and eat it, too. I actually said those words and then I explained myself.

I told him that I could bake him a cake (meaning that I'd do whatever he needed to be done) but that he couldn't also tell me how to bake it (meaning, the steps to get there). In other words, he could tell me what type of cake he wanted, but he couldn't tell me what ingredients to use. At first, he resisted. But then I heard him use the same analogy on one of our more challenging stakeholders while we were in a meeting together. After that, we had a completely different relationship. We came to an understanding that my job was to get him what he needed, and it felt like we were on the same team.

With this arrangement in place, that position turned out to be one of the most successful and influential roles I have ever had. My boss' grumpiness was a gift. It forced me to seek common ground so that we both got what we wanted.

WHAT YOU NEED TO KNOW!

We all feel the pressure to get results.

We're all asked to do things that don't deliver on those results.

We need to be mindful of the Illusion Point and avoid the Great Idea Cycle of Death.

We need to explain how all our wasted effort is in no one's best interest.

We have to push back on the requests that we know won't work.

Chapter 2:
YOUR COMPANY SUCKS

In the last chapter, we examined how leaders are often the source of the problem. They feel pressure to deliver results, so they ask us to do things but they also tell us how to perform those tasks. Those things don't deliver the results or have the impact the leaders expect and everyone involved gets frustrated.

Not all of the blame should fall on the boss, but as leaders, by definition, they have more organizational power and control than employees do. Also in the last chapter, we learned how too much control by leaders can lead to the counterproductive Illusion Point. So, how do we fix this Illusion Point?

Organizational charts, or org charts, have existed for more than a century and are a familiar aspect of any business model. The company org chart lays out, in the most basic visual terms, who is below us, who is above us, and who is beside us by connecting all leaders and employees through a series of neat, organized boxes and lines. Without the org chart, supposedly we would have no clue where employees sit within the greater hierarchy of the company.

Conceptually, org charts help us make business decisions by laying out who is in charge and who decides what we do. They tell us who we direct questions to, who we allocate tasks to, who will be impacted by the decisions we make, and who the decision makers are in the org chart above us. An org chart, by design, keeps office life organized and business running smoothly while also motivating those looking to advance their careers by encouraging competition among employees. A little competition between employees can certainly be a good thing; it can inspire new ideas and improve the quality of our work. But sometimes that backfires.

Because most org charts highlight a rigid top-down structure, they can create a cutthroat culture, which may bring out the worst in some of our coworkers, particularly those who care only about getting to the top. Those employees will do whatever's necessary to get ahead, even if it means forgoing teamwork for personal accomplishment. It's even worse when the employee focused only on moving up is the boss because his or her employees will take all the flak when things don't go the boss' way. When competition creates that type of work atmosphere, the quality of our work life inevitably suffers.

Another problem with the traditional org chart is that it almost exclusively encourages upward communication, since collaboration and communication with our peers come with the risk of giving them a leg up. Given the nature of the power structure, employees tend to see only the opportunity for vertical growth, leaving little reason to communicate good ideas with peers in other parts of the company. Sharing ideas puts our own recognition at risk.

It's human nature to want to please our bosses, just like we wanted to please our parents when we were growing up. It's also human nature to willingly step on our peers to gain that recognition. This is how teams and departments get siloed and lose efficiency.

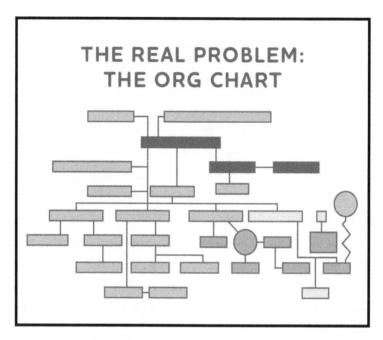

THE REAL PROBLEM: THE ORG CHART

In a vertical org chart, we tend to think less about what our peers in other parts of the company or our subordinates need from us and more about gaining individual recognition. This structure breaks down collaboration and initiative both downward and sideways. The traditional org chart, likely familiar, looks something like this.

On a positive note, the traditional org chart is clean and orderly. It's got some nice straight lines and evenly spaced bubbles and boxes.

I've been an employee in more than 50 different jobs and have worked closely with countless companies as a consultant, but I've never seen a company that fits the model laid out on the nice clean org chart. Things shake out much differently in the disruptive and innovative world in which we live today. Also, unspoken rules often contribute to the hierarchy of an organization.

If I were tasked with creating an org chart that accurately represents what goes on in a company between everyone who works there, one that details the complicated relationships and power structures that play out every day, I can imagine what that org chart would look like. At the top might be an executive who has a silent partner who really calls the shots. Maybe there is a senior VP who is having an affair with someone in the company that a few people know about. There are the inevitable secret crushes that can happen when you bring human beings together in any kind of organization.

There are always going to be people who just really don't like each other, some who can't let grudges go and refuse to settle old scores. That leads to secret resentments. There are the folks who support the same football team. There's the person who runs an office lottery. Plus, there might also be siblings or married couples working together at the company. You might have someone who sells drugs to other people. Don't forget about the group who plays golf together and those whose kids all go to the same school or church or play on the same baseball team. And you know the IT guy has some dirt on someone high up because it's a mystery that he hasn't been fired yet.

This likely sounds familiar to many of us. Maybe the org chart really looks like this:

In this example, what kind of boxes do these employees fit into, and what kind of lines need to connect them? When looking at any org chart, we can so easily forget that the boxes and lines are meant to represent real people who have families and who struggle with problems.

We are complicated. Our relationships are complicated, constantly in flux, and can change so quickly. As many of us know,

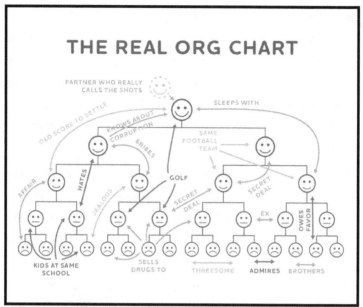

Image inspired by Integration Training (UK)ˣ.

it's difficult to navigate the typical office environment daily; it's never neat and orderly. To come up with a proper business plan, a company needs to recognize these realities. No org chart will accurately represent an authentic office environment because no series of lines and boxes can effectively encapsulate the human element.

THE MAGIC OF THE BULLSEYE

Another, arguably more significant, problem with the org chart is that it doesn't include the most important person in any business: The customer. It doesn't make sense not to include this essential aspect of any company. In a world where companies must prove to be customer-centric more than ever, this oversight is egregious. Businesses exist only because of their customers; therefore, no matter the department, all jobs are customer service jobs.

Why does the org chart matter? Employees may think, "It's just an org chart." That may seem true, but components like the org chart make up a company's culture. The impact on the individual employee may be small, but when looking at the bigger picture, the org chart contributes to and is an indicator of a company's misguided priorities.

The org chart is a good place to start when a company wants to shift the priority back to the customer. Employees from separate departments focus on the same goal and that brings an organization together. The org chart will show whether the company is serious about prioritizing the customer.

This is not as easy as it sounds, especially for large companies with many employees working on multiple projects at the same time. Departments inevitably become siloed over time. Redirecting a company's focus is like trying to turn around a giant ship; it's clunky and slow-moving.

It takes a lot of time, resources, and organization to realign several departmental goals back into a common one. Separate company departments have separate agendas. Predictably, departments end up working toward different goals for different bosses. However, when department goals diverge, it lessens the effectiveness of the company's products and ultimately its whole brand. Inefficiency seeps in between the silos and affects the business' bottom line.

How does a company motivate the various departments to work together? Does it rely on carrots and sticks? Does it take employee ideas and cram them in a box somewhere? Does it host brainstorming sessions and one-off design thinking workshops? Maybe it does casual Fridays or attempts to create camaraderie through trust-building sessions in the woods. Maybe it asks its employees to read a leadership book with a red cover.

Unfortunately, these ideas won't work. To truly foster a culture of empathy and prevent misguided or competing priorities, we first need to break the silos throughout our organizations. This means companies ensure that all departments focus their efforts on the customer, and all company goals keep the customer experience in mind. One simple way to accomplish that is to rethink the way the org chart is designed.

I call this new type of org chart design "the Bullseye."

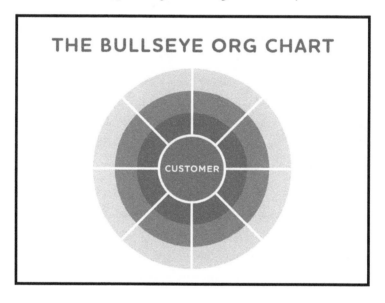

THE BULLSEYE ORG CHART

CUSTOMER

Simply put, the Bullseye reminds all employees why they're at work and who they need to serve. Because its design is a target instead of a vertically designed hierarchy, it breaks up tension between peers. It directs every employee's focus on the same center target point, motivating all employees to concentrate on the same goals and the same priority.

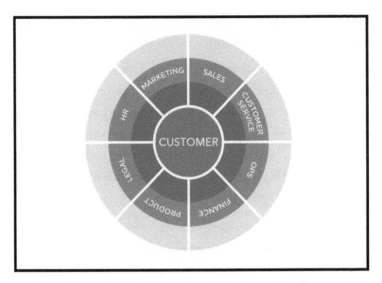

The Bullseye also promotes more communication flow in all directions, as opposed to encouraging cutthroat upward mobility. Using the Bullseye chart can shift how your company manages its goals and how it relates to its customers. As a result, the company's hierarchy becomes more unified. This real org chart becomes less political, less messy, and less difficult to navigate.

For companies that are being pulled in every direction, the Bullseye acts as a clarifying tool. It sets the standard for decisions made on every level by directing the decision-making to the same goal: Serving the customer. The Bullseye encourages employees to think of a customer as an individual so that they're not just seeing the customer as a bunch of statistics. That way, when it comes to brainstorming new ideas, we can more readily relate to our customer instead of taking a shot in the dark.

The Bullseye creates a culture of empathy and teamwork within the entire organization because all employees pull together to focus on serving others instead of themselves, their bosses, their secret allies, or the executive with a big ego. Bullseye org charts focus everyone on the common goal of serving the most important person to the organization, the customer.

As you can see, all departments including Marketing, Sales, Customer Service, HR, Operations, Finance, Product, and even Legal teams can use the Bullseye as a unifying force to align a company culture.

Implementing the Bullseye chart on its own provides no guarantee that your company's entire operation will shift its focus to your customer. I'm sure some of you are thinking: Yeah, but my company sucks. I'm not a CEO or the head of HR, so it's unlikely that they'll change the org chart because I suggested it or change our structure to focus on the customer at my request.

Fair enough. It's hard to change the tactics that have been ingrained in our company culture for such a long time. And it's even harder for ego-driven executives to listen to lower-level minions. Because, you know, the org chart.

While changing the company hierarchy may not be an immediate option, changing your own mindset or the way your team operates is certainly more doable. We may not think that's possible, but this book shares stories of people who have learned that it is. They were able to push back against controlling bosses, focus on the customer, and create a culture of empathy in their workplaces, even when they weren't the boss or CEO. It is possible, but it's not for the faint of heart.

MEAN CUSTOMERS SUCK, TOO!

Our bosses can be opinionated but our customers can be, too. When we put the customers at the focus of the Bullseye, we can't be surprised when those customers start speaking their minds.

They will have feedback and it will not always be good. To be honest, sometimes mean customers suck, too!

My close friend and marketing guru, Jay Baer, begins one of his speeches by playing an audio recording of an actor reading an infamous negative review of White Castle on TripAdvisor.

The review goes something like this: "I cannot believe that these people actually exchange real American currency for this square steamed mixture of rodent feces and sawdust on a tiny bun. This is the bastard love child of 7-11 microwavable meat patty and the entrail drippings of roadkill left to fester on Midwestern highways in the hot July sun. Happily, it's as thin as a Post-it Note, so as not to inadvertently engage your gag reflex."

Our natural reaction is to ignore a review like this. But as Jay explains in his book, *Hug Your Haters*[xi], that is the worst possible thing you can do because it makes a bad situation worse. Not answering customer complaints tells the customer that you don't care about them or their issues. "The customer isn't always right, but the customer should always be heard," is the way Jay puts it when encouraging employees to answer every complaint in every channel every time to turn a positive into a negative.

DON'T SHY AWAY FROM
CONSTRUCTIVE CRITICISM

In April of 2018, I received an email from Alicia Haugen. It turns out that she had purchased my first book, The Content Formula, as well as the Marketing ROI calculator we sold along with it. But there was a problem: One of the formulas didn't work. When I saw her email, I immediately issued her a refund. I contacted my developer to fix the issue, and we made the calculator free for everyone until it was fixed.

Alicia then went on social media and created an amazing testimonial video of the whole situation. She complimented my developer and me for our rapid response and attention to her issues. I never asked her to tell everyone how we tried to make the best of a bad situation, but that's what she did.

If we focus on our customers and listen to what they have to say, we'll encourage a positive feedback loop: They'll let us in on a problem, we'll listen accordingly, and then act when necessary. The power that comes along with a customer-centric approach isn't limited to bettering your product, it also brings in new customers. We don't have to tell customers that we're the best; we can listen to their concerns and show them we care by acting on the issues. Whenever possible, we should adjust our products or services according to customer feedback.

As a leader, changing long-held habits and perspectives to better the customer experience is tricky. Leaders like Jay recognize that in order to establish future success at their companies, or for their clients, they need to get their hands dirty. They need to do whatever work they can to better the customer experience and put the customer at the center of the Bullseye.

THE MISSION STATEMENT

Satya Nadella learned the importance of empathy when, at 29, his wife prematurely gave birth to their son who weighed only three pounds and suffered from severe brain damage and cerebral palsy[xii] .

His first reaction was the obvious one, the one we'd all probably have if we were in that situation: Why did this happen to us? Over time, Nadella's perspective shifted, and he realized the real person who was wronged in this situation was his son, not him. He wrote in his autobiography, Hit Refresh, "It was time for me to step up and see life through his eyes and do what I should do as a parent and father."

That lesson in empathy remained with Nadella when he took over as Microsoft CEO in 2014. Nadella felt that the culture of Microsoft needed to change. He wanted to turn the company from a "know-it-all" culture to a "learn-it-all" one. He told managers that "no one ever learns through criticism," and he set out to create a "soul" for the organization.

Before I work with a new client, I look at their mission statement. If their website proudly brags, "We are the leading provider of widgets in the world," then I know that this is not an empathetic company and it needs to define its marketing mission. While I have helped more than a dozen companies define their marketing missions, only a few of those companies have used that exercise as a model to change their entire approach to communicating.

The model I use is simple. What does the company do for its customers? What benefit does the company provide? What problem does the company solve?

Nadella recognized that they needed more empathy at Microsoft. He started by crafting a new mission statement that put people before products:

To empower every person and every organization on the planet to achieve more.

Nadella's leadership style put the company focus back on the customer and helped lead a huge turnaround for the tech giant. It has also led to the creation of numerous innovations that have come out of Microsoft over the last few years. Nadella's customer-centric leadership even earned him the title of Fortune's Most Underrated CEO three years in a row[xiii] .

Is Microsoft the greatest place in the world to work? I'm not sure. I know a few dozen Microsoft employees and they talk about a culture that empowers employees and truly does focus on innovations that help people. They also talk about how Microsoft might have leadership challenges like most companies do and that they still need to work hard on hiring and promoting leaders who embody their core values. So, no, they're not perfect.

But if you had a choice to work for the world's leading widget maker or the company whose CEO talks about the power of empathy and having a mission of improving people's lives, which would you choose? I think most of us would prefer to work for the executive and the company that places a focus on empathy.

What is your company mission statement? If your org chart doesn't include customers, what about the mission statement? How can employees focus on customers if the mission of the company doesn't even mention them? A company should be focused on the people it serves, not just on its internal operations. Therefore, its mission statement shouldn't tell only what the company does, but it should also prioritize for whom it's being done.

The mission statement acts as a guide to the company's goals and its brand. Without proper attention paid to the customer, the company ends up relegating its most important person to the bottom of the barrel. Ensure that the goals of your company are focused on the customer by including what you can do for the customer in its fundamental formula.

As an example, we can look at this simple mission statement from an imaginary burger joint:

Best Burger makes the best burgers in the city.

This mission statement says only what the restaurant does by stating what the internal operations accomplish. It tells diners that the company aims to make the best burgers in the city. It screams, "We are awesome!" However, customer service is a huge part of being a successful burger joint, so wouldn't the restaurant want to include that portion of its business in its mission statement? Without it, it lacks the recognition it deserves.

The burger joint then creates this revised mission statement:

Best Burger serves hungry Philadelphians the best burgers in the city.

It seems like a simple change and to some degree it is. As with the simple changes made to a company org chart, the impact of small adjustments of this kind to a mission statement gives a company a head start in changing its culture. Simply acknowledging the customer in the equation changes the direction in which the business' thinking goes. This revised mission statement illustrates what the restaurant does and what it does for its customers; that small adjustment will echo through the company branding and through its employees when they think about how to best accomplish the company's mission.

I think about my 50+ jobs and wonder, in how many of them did I pay attention to the company mission statement? I walked out of that pizza restaurant job after watching four hours of video in a closet, likely because one of those videos talked about how I needed to help the company become the best pizza joint in the world. I don't recall it being a conscious choice but I remember it.

I held a job later in my career that I don't like to talk about; I was there for only a few weeks. The company didn't have a mission statement, but the CEO probably would have said, "Our mission is to make money." I didn't consciously think about the company mission statement (or lack thereof). I did notice that my desk chair at that company was outdated and very uncomfortable. I also saw that the company didn't care about customers, employees, laws, or ethics; it cared only about making money.

Companies that innovate and grow know what their customers want because they put resources into understanding what their customers care about—the very definition of organizational empathy. They know how to put their customers first by understanding their preferences and being true to their mission as a business. Successful companies understand that they must stick to the script they used to get those customers to begin with. What their customers value in their business is what they should be promoting to the world. What results from sticking to a core message is a business with goals and motives that feel genuine to consumers.

When I run workshops with clients, the first thing we do is create a more customer-focused mission using this simple formula:

- Who do we serve?
- What problem do we solve?
- What impact does that make?

Based on that formula, my Best Burger company mission statement is not yet completely empathetic. We use the formula to revise it:

Best Burger makes Philadelphians happy by filling their bellies with good food.

That's it. The mission statement is complete.

It all comes down to the experience we give the customers that we serve. It's not about what we do as a company; it's about why we do it. We think about what our business was founded on; we realize that what our company values most deeply is likely what our customers also value most deeply. We run with that. When we find a message and a mission statement that sticks, customer loyalty will follow.

THE PERILS OF IGNORING
CUSTOMER DEMAND

The story of Kodak offers one of the best examples of what a company should not do. The story may be familiar, but Larry Matteson and his part in the Kodak story may not be. The camera phone might not exist if it weren't for Larry, and his little-known story can guide us all.

Before camera phones, a Kodak disposable camera was the popular camera. For a long time, the disposable camera was the go-to tool of the amateur photographer in the predigital era. Before we could take selfies with our smartphones, we'd have to turn the plastic camera around toward our faces, aim blindly, and hope for the best. Lighting was always an issue and uncorrectable red eye made for many regrettable pictures. Then, we'd have to drive to our local convenience store and wait for an hour to get those blurry, red-eye photos developed. Still, this process was exciting in its own way—waiting to have the photos printed created a certain ritual that forced us to relive the memories on the film once we had them in our hands.

Kodak led the way in the film and camera industry for decades. In the US market, Kodak's success in the industry was unparalleled. In 1976[xiv] , Kodak made up nearly 85 percent of all camera sales in the US. Though business success was stable, it translated into a false sense of security within the company. Eventually, digital cameras transformed the industry, and Kodak would have no way to battle the rapid-fire change in the industry they dominated for so long.

Even in the age of the smartphone with its ever-evolving camera abilities, Kodak remains a household name. The disposable camera may have lost its stronghold on the photography and film markets long ago but it still brings back plenty of nostalgia. We might pass out disposable cameras at weddings as a fun twist or use them sporadically for vintage-quality photos.

Although a retro boom is happening for certain items, like disposable cameras and vinyl records that have been lost to newer technologies, unfortunately for Kodak that resurgence didn't happen soon enough. Post digital camera, the company couldn't bring in the level of revenue that would keep them highly profitable. In January 2012, with hundreds of thousands of employees, Kodak filed for Chapter 11 protection from bankruptcy. That same year, Facebook bought Instagram and its dozen or so employees for one billion dollars. The revolutionary photograph technology that Kodak created in the 1970s and 1980s was rendered nearly obsolete by our world's digital transformation.

The company's saga is a familiar one across many industries. It just couldn't adapt its technology quickly enough to compete with other businesses producing digital cameras. For years, the company's sales revenue dipped as the popularity in new digital image technology rose. However, it's possible that those dips didn't have to fall as far as they did. Some employees at Kodak saw the downturn coming. Some predicted that the company would take a big hit. Kodak's decline could have been mitigated with the right response had one employee been listened to more carefully.

In 1979, Larry Matteson was an executive at Kodak. He wrote a report examining how the market could potentially shift, given recent technological advancements in digital photography. Larry predicted with stunning accuracy that digital photography would start by being adopted by the government. He said it would then move into corporate surveillance, followed by professional photographers, and would ultimately become a daily consumer tool. In 1979, Larry predicted exactly how the digital mobile revolution would unfold and its impact on Kodak. But Kodak's other executives failed to take the warning seriously enough to spur any immediate or significant action.

Sure enough, as public demand shifted, Kodak saw its position as a billion-dollar industry stalwart fade into the past. An end to their success seemed impossible, so it's understandable why Kodak resisted change. The company had been so successful for so long and had dominated the industry for what seemed like an eternity; to abandon its business models seemed inconceivable. Although Kodak had all the warning it needed from Larry, it still allowed the org chart to kill the company.

Many companies have suffered a similar fate as Kodak. Customer expectations are rapidly changing, so it's becoming more and more difficult to cater to customers. Unfortunately, the nature of that change has turned the already existing gap between company and customer into an ever-expanding chasm.

Putting the customer at the center of the Bullseye and focusing on what consumers really want will help companies avoid being left behind.

WHAT YOU NEED TO KNOW!

Companies are messy because people are messy, so the traditional org chart doesn't accurately capture the structure of any real company.

Rethink the nature of the org chart by adapting the Bullseye and putting the customer at the center. This will shift the focus company-wide and get every department keyed in on a common goal.

Listen to your customers and their complaints. Don't ignore your customers. Address their concerns head on.

The same way the org chart needs to focus on the customer so does your mission statement. What a company does is not as important as why they do it and who they do it for.

When you're in tune with your employees and the ever-changing wants and challenges of the customer, you will be equipped to adapt when a cultural shift occurs.

Chapter 3:
YOUR MANAGER SUCKS

For all of you who think that you can't make a difference or influence change because you aren't the CEO, this story is for you.

My son is obsessed with LEGOs®. If you ask his classmates what his favorite thing in the world is, they will all tell you that it's LEGOs. And it is partly thanks to LEGOs that he says he wants to grow up and become an engineer. How cool is that?

"LEGO" is a combination of the two Danish words leg godt, which means "play well." It started as a wooden toy company in the 1930s and has been selling its blockbuster little plastic bricks since 1949. According to Lego.com, nearly a trillion LEGOs have been sold, making it one of the most popular toys in the world.

But in the late 1990s, LEGO was on the brink of a Kodak-style bankruptcy[xv]. It had layoffs and millions of dollars of debt and almost didn't survive. Today, LEGO is one of the most recognized, innovative, and customer-focused brands in the world. So, how did it turn things around?

LEGO tapped into something I call Champion Leadership. It had brought Jorgen Vig Knudstorp onto the team as a junior consultant in 2001. A father of four children, like me, he eventually rose to become CEO of the company just three years later making him the first non-family member to become CEO of this closely held family-run empire. How did he get there?

Becoming the CEO didn't happen without Jorgen taking some big risks. Even as a new employee, he told his higher-ups that the company was flailing and would eventually fail because its rapid expansion had led to precarious finances that would only get worse. Like Larry at Kodak, Jorgen started looking around for ideas. He spent two years talking to employees and customers.

In 2003, he asked for a meeting with the senior leaders of the company to tell them that the end was near: LEGO was losing nearly one million dollars a day. He further pointed out that the company had too many products. Even though it made only one thing (plastic bricks of various colors, shapes, and sizes), it had 14,000 suppliers (more suppliers than Boeing, a company that makes entire airplanes). The company was losing too much money, he said, and he believed the situation was going to get much worse. He then said these famous words:

"We are on a burning platform, losing money, with negative cash flow and a real risk of debt default. Which could lead to a breakup of the company."

He walked out of the office that day and called his wife to say that he thought he would be fired. No leader wants to hear that his or her company is floundering, especially from a junior consultant. Many of the leaders on the management team just didn't believe Jorgen's predictions, and they denied that they had made the very mistakes that got them there.

But Jorgen was not fired. Instead, the CEO at the time, the

grandson of founder, Ole Kirk Christiansen, named him CEO of the company! Though he was only 35 years old and inexperienced as a leader of a business that size, he took the challenge head on. As the new CEO, Jorgen immediately pushed back against the company's debt, cutting costs vigorously until the company turned a profit again.

Jorgen's vision for bringing the company back to life centered on empathy. He accomplished this by studying children as they played with LEGO's signature bricks. He brought in psychologists to study children at play. He even asked his designers to spend a week living with families of children who liked playing with LEGOs to learn how they built and unbuilt LEGOs. He also instructed them to learn how children "played well" together. By sticking to the company's core customer base and its original successful message, LEGO adapted to the changing business landscape without going under.

The fact that Jorgen Vig Knudstorp could rise from junior consultant to CEO because he delivered the bad news the leaders needed to hear is a testament to the benefits of listening to employees and taking risks. However, Jorgen isn't the true hero of this story.

When, as a junior consultant, he showed the executives that a good CEO sees the company as it is, not as he wishes it to be, the *executive team* should be credited for believing that Jorgen could be that CEO. When he asked *his designers* to bring in psychologists to better understand children at play or to go live for a week with families to learn about children's behavior, the designers should get some credit for trusting this inexperienced CEO with the future of their company. And when *his marketing team* came up with the idea[xvi] to make a movie about LEGOs and to start crowdsourcing new LEGO concepts to customers with the chance of getting a percentage of the profits, these marketers and his CFO should get the credit for trusting in Jorgen's goals of using empathy and focusing on customers first to save their company.

His leadership team and the employees around him truly exemplified what it means to be a Champion Leader because they recognized the value in his research and his vision. They championed his ideas to correct the problems they hadn't yet figured out how to solve. In turn, they started to see how empathy and a customer focus delivered ideas and innovations that brought the company back from the brink of destruction.

Just imagine the courage (or desperation) of the executive board to recognize the leadership skills and trust the judgment of an inexperienced employee well below them in the hierarchy. If Knudstorp's superiors fired him and didn't champion his ideas, LEGO probably wouldn't be around or at least it certainly wouldn't be what it is today. It would be another Kodak story.

If you manage people at work, think long and hard about how well you champion your employees' ideas, if you report to a manager you love, it's likely because that manager encourages your ideas and supports them to his or her peers.

If you are an executive, this is the most important job you have. According to a study of more than 400,000[xvii] people, one trait led them to work harder and it was more important than salary, benefits, or perks. These hard-working employees believed that it was most important when promotions, raises, bonuses, and praise were handed out fairly.

Show me a happy employee and chances are their ideas are being championed at work and they are being treated fairly. But how do we take this a step further and get entire organizations to follow this model of Champion Leadership?

HARNESS POTENTIAL THROUGH EMPLOYEE ACTIVATION

Imagine if we could activate our smartest and most driven employees to focus on fixing the biggest challenges in our organizations? Imagine the potential if more organizations were staffed by a team of experts like Jorgen, who were skilled and driven by a real focus on adding value to their customers. What a powerhouse a company could be if its employees were recognized as passionate thought leaders!

Luckily, you're already sitting on this golden egg. Whether you know it or not, your employees are skilled experts with their own unique and valuable beliefs, perspectives, and insights. How can you harness that potential? Unfortunately, you won't be able to turn your employees into your industry's dream team overnight because many employees have been conditioned to keep their ideas to themselves out of fear of repercussion.

According to Gallup, only three out of every 10 employees feel that their opinions matter at work. Dr. Amy Edmondson, a professor at Harvard, refers to workers' perceived ability to speak their minds and give input as "psychological safety[xviii]." Mastering a culture that promotes psychological safety can transform a stagnant work culture into one where employees are deeply engaged with one another. It also trains employees to explore new ways of thinking, and when employees know that they can offer ideas without facing negative consequences if the ideas don't work, the creative juices will flow.

Fostering a culture of psychological safety is only half the battle to getting employees engaged at work. To really get the most out of our employees, we need to do more than just listen to them when they propose ideas. We need to take their ideas to the next step. While psychological safety allows for more experimental idea expression, it doesn't execute those good ideas.

Showing employees that their input makes a measurable difference requires some action on a manager's part. It requires relinquishing control and empowering employees to share their expertise. It's about giving them a secure platform, supporting and encouraging them to express themselves through their own personal brand, which, in turn, comes back as a positive reflection on the company brand. The process of putting employees' ideas into action isn't a sales, marketing, or communications technique as much as it is a shift in organizational culture that will stretch the reach of the company. The company can then engage, inspire, and retain customers on a whole new level.

To reach this goal, a manager should:

• Keep an "open door."

• Spend time with lower-level employees.

• Be constantly on the search for new innovations.

• Look for inspiration from other teams.

These are the steps prescribed by Trish Mueller, formerly Home Depot's advertising VP and CMO, who says that she makes herself as approachable as possible to employees so that they feel comfortable coming to her with any issues they may face on the job.

"You never know where the next innovation may come from, and you'll never hear it unless you dig in with the team," she told *Ad Age* in a 2016 interview[xix].

Every company has a Larry Matteson (Kodak), but too few have a Jorgen Vig Knudstorp (LEGO) or a Trish Mueller (Home Depot) because few employees work in an environment where their ideas are championed. Big ideas often get lost when we don't encourage employees to voice their input. The innovative risk-takers of our companies are indispensable in keeping our businesses moving forward—they're the groundbreakers, the renegades, and the creatives.

Leaders who champion their employees' ideas, like Knudstorp's bosses and team at LEGO, show empathy for the people who work for them. They also see multiple business improvements:

1. **Championing employee ideas creates more job appreciation among employees.** People are generally happier at work when leaders value their input and make that known. Research conducted by Glassdoor[xx] found employees consider "culture and values" to be the most important aspects of their job. Company culture even bested salary as the best predictor of job satisfaction for employees. Leaders who value people over process are far more likely to have loyalty among employers, too. When we're unhappy at work, we don't quit our jobs, we quit our bosses.

2. **One employee's championed idea opens the door for others to feel comfortable expressing their big ideas.** When more employees share their thoughts, better collaboration among teams occurs. One idea might start a snowball of ideas from others in brainstorming sessions. Meetings that previously included too much dead silence will instead promote conversation and critical

discussion. Companies that value letting employees express their ideas—even their most ridiculous ones—end up winning the game of creativity. And for the companies that value innovation and creative brainstorming, this is important.

3. **Employees who feel like valued members of the company, and not just salary earners, are more likely to have engaging conversations with customers.** Word of mouth happens naturally when an empowered employee engages with customers; it's only as powerful as the voice that word is coming from.

Change can take time, so we can't afford to wait around for those other companies to wake up. Today is the day for managers to ask, measure, and track employee sentiments so that managers can see where employees could improve and then learn how to empower them. Employees might have great ideas that their managers would have never even considered. When employees are engaged, inspired, and motivated, the impact of their positivity and expertise is mind-blowing!

Of course, it's unreasonable to think that leaders will be able to invest in every big idea that's presented to them. They won't, and they shouldn't. Having empathy for our employees doesn't mean going along with every big idea—it means listening, being open to those big ideas when they come, and supporting the ones that have a real chance to change the game.

MEAN EMPLOYEES SUCK!

I hear this declaration from leaders constantly: "If only my team would execute my strategy. The reason we're struggling is because

we don't hire and train better people." It sounds like an excuse because it is. A leader who makes excuses and blames his or her team
doesn't deserve the moniker of "leader." However, occasionally an
employee's skills or motivations don't line up with the direction
that a business or the rest of the team is headed. What should
managers do if one of their employees sucks?

While performance can sometimes be tricky to gauge, attitude is
not. Most employees who suck, suck because they are mean. They
likely disrupt meetings, make inappropriate comments, bully others, or mansplain. They use subtle ways to subjugate lower-level
employees, women, or diverse populations. When employees treat
others with disrespect, that behavior can become so much more
toxic than many managers realize. Mean employees suck, and
managers simply have no good reason to keep them.

Sometimes situations force a manager to make the difficult decision to fire an employee who is a genuinely good person and a
hard worker. At 28 years old, I was asked to manage my first team
and on that team was a great guy, "Eric." I liked Eric a lot. He was
a little older than I was and had been hired by my predecessor
because he had thought that Eric had the skills and experience
the company needed. But the client Eric was hired to serve com-
plained about his performance.

I first gave Eric the benefit of the doubt and issued him a warning to address the client's concerns. Eric listened and agreed to
improve. I knew that to create a culture of empathy, a good leader
must have patience with performance issues and work with the
individuals involved so there is no confusion. That's what I did
and had hoped the issue was solved. But a month later, the client
said there was no improvement at all. For the first time in my life,
I had to fire someone and the last person I wanted to fire was Eric.

Firing someone is never easy, but when employees are toxic, managers must get rid of them immediately. As illustrated earlier in the survey of 400,000 people, fairly managing praise, promotions, and pay is one of the most important jobs managers have. Company culture is set by who gets hired and fired (or not). When managers don't fire an employee who is toxic, they are telling their organization that the bad behavior is okay.

Sometimes, a mismatch in skills or expectations happens. Eric was a nice person but he wasn't a match for the position, so I had to let him go. It was a decision I initially fought, but in the long run it paid off for both parties. Eric went on to find a job he loved where he excelled and made a real impact. As this example shows, if an employee isn't a good fit for the company culture or a particular position, the manager has no reason to keep the employee. Good, hard-working people like Eric will find a place out there for them. Sometimes letting them go is the first step in helping them find that better opportunity.

IS IT POSSIBLE TO FOSTER INNOVATION?

Research conducted by McKinsey & Company[xxi] shows that 70 percent of senior executives say innovation is a top priority within their business, yet many leaders don't feel confident in their ability to make decisions around innovation. As leaders, championing employee ideas can fill that knowledge gap. The Champion Leader supports and bolsters employee innovation.

In the digital era, innovation has become a hallmark of success but it is tricky to manufacture. It's one of the most sought-after workplace characteristics in today's business climate but continual innovation doesn't come easily for most. Our brains need specific, optimal conditions for creativity to happen.

When we really need to be creative and think outside the box, generating new ideas can seem even more challenging than usual. Writer's block hits. Brainstorming sessions result in blank white boards. We get stuck because creativity thrives on the spontaneous, the unexpected, and on having the freedom to fail. Structure, organization, and process—elements that a company must embrace to survive—tend to quash the creative spark in us. Fostering a workplace that maintains innovation and creativity as top priorities requires valuing employee values, rather than actions.

Innovation is hard to initiate and laborious to implement. Developing an innovative idea into a reality takes time—sometimes years. But even harder is maintaining innovation once an organization is known for it. Once expectations become built into an organization's thinking, the pressure to be creative is overpowering.

According to *Psychology Today*[xxii], our brains only want to be creative when they're in "safe spaces." That means all the other tasks that cause us to stress and worry—the more practical parts of our jobs—hinder our ability to make time for creativity. It's a similar concept to a sports team that's riding an undefeated streak: Once they've started winning, the only thing left is to lose. The overwhelming pressure to keep winning makes the game even more challenging.

To foster innovation at work, we need to work for a company that rewards values as opposed to actions. The best way to set that standard and make it clear to everyone is through who the company chooses to hire, fire, and promote. We see how our companies handle promotions at work and that, maybe more clearly than anything, signals to us what the company values. To foster more innovation among our employees, leaders need to signal to employees that innovation is what's expected and rewarded. Inc. reported on one study that included more than 40,000 participants on motivation in the workplace. According to Inc. Magazine[xvi], the biggest motivating factor for employees was the belief that promotions were managed effectively.

Companies that value only actions tend to promote employees who only go through the motions. These employees don't take risks; they only follow instructions and likely kiss up to their bosses. This type of company culture boosts up the people who simply check the boxes and do as their bosses tell them to, not questioning why they're completing certain tasks. They do as they're told even when they might disagree with the boss' strategy. That approach encourages employees to keep those big ideas to themselves because they won't risk upsetting their bosses.

As Champion Leaders, we want to promote and hire based on values and certain desirable traits, like innovative thinking. That will help to solidify a culture of innovation while eliminating much of the cutthroat politics and drama that can rot the average workplace from the inside out. We want to hire and promote the people who are the best fit for the job and the culture, not just the people who will say yes to a boss' every whim while trying to push other coworkers further down the ladder.

All of this does not come without risk. It requires leaders to put a lot of faith and trust in their employees to create customer-centric content, solve problems, and come up with innovative ideas. However, if you trust the people you promote and hire and they share the same values, you can trust that the culture you created will serve as a support system that ultimately limits your risk.

COMPANIES CAN NEVER STOP LEARNING

As start-up culture flourished years ago, General Electric (GE) realized it needed to try something new to remain competitive. While smaller companies were already capitalizing on various new ideas, GE knew it couldn't pour resources into projects that were going to be duds. The company therefore set out to foster more innovation among its employees.

Jeffrey Immelt, the company's CEO at the time, felt strongly about creating a culture at GE that more closely resembled that of start-ups. Immelt looked at Silicon Valley and saw that start-up mentality allowed for production to happen quickly on new ideas. He wanted that combination of creativity and speed to become a bigger part of GE's culture, so GE developed a program called FastWorks[xxiii].

Immelt hired entrepreneur Eric Ries to oversee the implementation of the FastWorks program, which he had modeled after the examples laid out in Ries' book, *The Startup Way*. The core concept behind the program was to foster more creativity and innovation among employees and in doing so, allow GE to generate more new ideas in a short amount of time. It would then be ready to quickly implement the best ideas without resorting to the prolonged development process they currently used. That type of efficiency would put GE even with the competing companies on the start-up stage.

Before implementing the new program, it would have taken

GE years to come up with a new idea because the old process required so much time for building and perfecting that idea. With FastWorks, the plan was to cut down that process time to a year or less. After the product was ready to go to the customer, GE teams would surely have to make tweaks. Now, recreating a product's design to fit customer needs—even if it took six, seven, eight tries—was all part of the process. It seemed risky, but leadership knew that championing new employee ideas, while giving those employees the flexibility to think outside the box, would take the company to the next level.

This was a big move for a huge company, but it worked because it focused on the customer. GE showed its commitment to the customer by ensuring that customer feedback was implemented shortly after the first product release. The program also promoted new employee ideas and encouraged more input in the decision-making process. The ancillary benefit was that by keeping the customer in the center of their planning, GE was also able to create efficient products more quickly.

Employees needed some time to trust in the cultural transition within the company, but they quickly learned that their leaders wanted them to feel empowered and encouraged their input. Because this new program utilized the ideas and innovation of all employees, not just the so-called innovative employees, it worked.

HELP EMPLOYEES HELP THEMSELVES

When Steve Lucas became the CEO of Marketo, now an Adobe company, one of his earliest initiatives was to put Kristen Kaighn in charge of employee engagement for the entire company. (Coincidentally, Kristen lives and grew up near me, so I was thrilled to hear her story when we spoke in November 2017.) At the time that Steve joined Marketo, Kristen was a marketing employee, so why did Steve task her with getting the entire company engaged?

As new CEO, Steve looked around the organization and noticed that the employees were not as engaged as he was. (In truth, few people are as pumped about anything as he is. His energy is electric and infectious.) He saw programs that focused on generating revenue, but he didn't see many programs focused on employees. It became Kristen's job to change that.

Up to that point, Marketo had offered its employees some perks, such as purple hoodies when they joined the company, purple onesies when they had babies, and free donuts and coffee. But maybe it hadn't truly considered what its employees were interested in. Kristen wanted to find that balance between what the company wanted, what the customers wanted, and what the employees wanted.

Kristen started by talking with the employees. She learned that they were open to engaging with the Marketo brand but only through authentic employee participation. She developed a platform, not because Steve wanted it done and not because the customers were interested in it, but because Kristen saw it as a way for the Marketo employees to help themselves. Through this platform, employees could grow their connections, build their personal brand, and propel their careers.

Kristen put together a truly empathetic objective to emotionally engage every employee with a purpose that was bigger than simply trying to sell more software. The engagement platform focused on the entire employee journey. The company developed a philosophy of producing content that touched the "head, hearts, and hands" of the people who worked there. It offered access to different events, cultural programs, community opportunities, and recruitment promotions, and even provided strategies to help the employees achieve their goals within the company.

Amazingly, Kristen was able to achieve nearly 100 percent participation while truly engaging 65 percent of the employees, twice as high as the average engagement percentage, as reported in the Gallup survey. Also, employee-referral hires increased 31 percent and significantly reduced company recruitment costs in the competitive talent markets of San Mateo, California, and Denver, Colorado. Additionally, the content created and shared by employees generated a 30 percent click-through rate (CTR) for every employee social share, which was 10 times the company average before creating the platform.

Kristen succeeded not only in engaging the employees—she created a program that helped HR, marketing, and the entire company. The lesson I learned from Kristen's amazing success is that simply focusing on customers is not enough. It's an important first step but it's not the only step. A successful company also focuses on employees. It shows its employees what's in it for them if they can demonstrate growth and innovation for the company and its customers. If an employer takes care of its employees, they will take care of their employer's business. Kristen realized something truly powerful: the employees were the greatest asset inside the organization.

Kristen left Marketo in October of 2018. She is now leading Global Customer Experience for Peakon, an employee feedback and data analytics platform, with the charge of helping other com-

panies like Marketo get the insights they need to improve employee engagement, build a strong company culture, and drive
business performance.

The Marketo employees I know personally are some of the
smartest, most passionate, engaged, and committed people I have
ever met. It starts with the energy from their leader, Steve Lucas,
but I also believe that Kristen's work helped set up the company
for its success.

As leaders, we can activate our employees: Convince them to
share what they know and what they love because it will help them
get what they want. This is one of the hottest areas of growth for
my own firm. Why pay an agency to create content when you can
activate the creators inside your company? Why pay an agency
to share stuff on social media when you can activate your own
employees to share interesting content, personal stories, and edu-
cational articles that attract like-minded people to your business?

CHAMPIONING EMPLOYEES
LEADS TO RESULTS

Two years ago, I was asked to present at an HR conference. As
I thought about what a marketing consultant would have to say
to HR people, I realized that HR and marketing are more related
than I'd first thought. Rather, marketing and HR are more related
than we could ever imagine.

In preparation for the event, I reached out to the CEOs of some
of the companies that would be present at the conference. When
I asked them to name the best example of a company that cham-

pions their employees, the answer I heard most often was Xenium HR. I then contacted the CEO of Xenium HR to understand why this company was so well known for being a leader in its field.

Xenium HR is a growing business outside Portland, Oregon that provides local employers with HR expertise and employer program solutions. According to its president, Anne Donovan, the company already had a great culture but it wanted to create an "integrated talent experience." It strived to hire employees who were happy and engaged from the day they were contacted about a new job opening until long after they had left the company. Xenium wanted people to love working there, so Anne's team created a program called the Xenium Culture Integration & Team Enhancement (XCITE).

The team gathered all the company employees and conducted surveys. They brainstormed and had lots of conversations to figure out how to create this integrated talent experience for all employees. The idea was to test this new program in-house before deciding whether to develop the program for customers.

They started by redefining their mission statement, and it's one that I love: "To develop great employers." Isn't that what we expect to be true for all HR professionals? Isn't that why they do what they do? Do many HR professionals think of this as their mission? I once overheard an HR manager say, "I can't fix crazy. But I can document it." Sadly, that sentiment captures how some HR professionals think of their job.

HR teams need to manage numerous tasks, such as recruiting, benefits, payroll, risk mitigation, compliance, and retirement solutions. These tasks are the ingredients needed to bake the cake that their customers are looking for: To become a great employer.

To reach that goal, Anne challenged her team with a manifesto:

Everyone works.

But not everyone loves their work.

And that's why we're here to change the game.

We help our clients grow.

Grow their people, their capabilities, their business.

And we do it by creating workplaces

where employers and employees can make a difference.

Better culture, shared values, real results—these are things we can bring to the table.

Because with the right environment, employees and employers thrive.

Managers become inspired leaders.

Employees excel in their jobs.

Businesses continue to grow.

This is why we're transforming the workplace.

For employees. For employers. For you.

Xenium celebrates its people on its website and in its mission statement: "Our people are our greatest gifts. We're passionate and purposeful about our work, and we encourage entrepreneurial thinking and leadership at every level of our organization."

Xenium took the insights gained from its own project and used them to create the HR services and solutions it offers its customers. Xenium wouldn't have done that if the project hadn't worked. According to Anne, the company has a better than 90 percent retention rate! That is much higher than average in its industry.

Xenium's HR consulting business is the driver of growth for its entire company. It transformed internally, created massive growth, and is reportedly very happy. Wouldn't we also be happy if we could talk about our businesses in the same way?

Xenium defined what they believed in. They defined their values and ideals because that's what matters to them. It's why they do what they do.

THE ONE-QUESTION SURVEY

I was an English Literature major in college, so it was the first business book I ever read that actually inspired my entire career. The book, *The Service Profit Chain,* by James L. Heskett, W. Earl Sasser, Jr., and Leonard A. Schlesinger, was published over 20 years ago (Free Press, 1997). Even then, the authors found that companies with engaged employees were more productive, had higher customer retention, and experienced significantly higher revenue growth. The authors showed that engaged employees created happy customers who drive share prices up. In other words, the employee experience drives everything.

In his book, *Grow: How Ideals Power Growth and Profit at the World's Greatest Companies,* Jim Stengel, the former CMO at Procter & Gamble, elaborates on his theory that companies that focus on improving people's lives see much higher growth (Crown Publishing Group, 2011). He found 50 different companies that valued their employees and were public examples of purpose-driven programs, strategies, missions, and go-to market tactics. He then tracked their stock price performance in the Fortune 500 and the S&P 500. He learned that those companies had almost 400 percent higher growth.

The concepts from these two awesome books inspired me to do my own research. I had a theory, a hypothesis that I wanted to test: Happy employees have Champion Leader managers who create an environment for growth and innovation. I fielded a random sample survey to gather data from over 2,000 employed people in the United States. I asked them three questions:

1. Are you happy at work?

2. Is the company you work for growing and innovative?

3. Does your manager champion your ideas?

From over 2,000 employed people surveyed, I found:

- Only 2% of them loved their jobs!

- As much as 8% hated their jobs (four times as many as those who loved them!).

- Approximately 45% either liked or disliked their jobs.

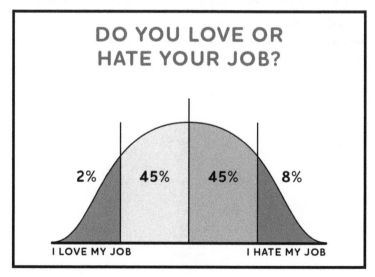

- Also, 77% of that 2% of people who loved their jobs had a manager who championed their ideas.

- And 50% of that 8% of people who hated their jobs did not have a manager who championed their ideas.

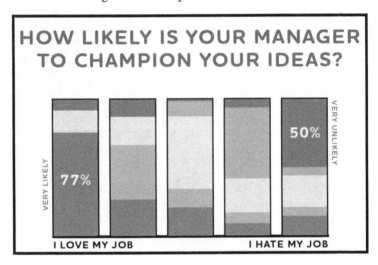

I also wondered about innovation. Do those happy employees with Champion Leader managers tend to work at innovative companies? Yes, they do!

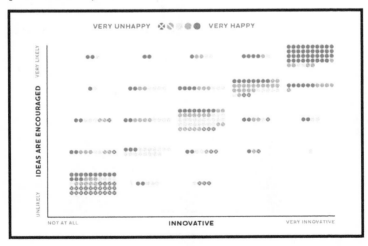

This chart shows that, as reported in the survey, the happiest employees have managers who champion their ideas and they also work at innovative companies.

From this survey, we can conclude that most of the happiest employees live in the world of Champion Leaders at innovative companies. Most of the unhappy employees are unlikely to have managers who support them or jobs in innovative companies. Further, not one employee reported the absence of idea encouragement and happiness while also reporting a job in an innovative company. I didn't find a single person who felt that he or she worked at an innovative company and didn't have a manager who supported his or her ideas. Not one. These results prove that the key to growth and innovation as a company is the same as the key to having happy employees and innovation: Employ people managers who champion the ideas of their team. The bottom line:

- If you want to be happy at work, find a manager who champions your ideas.

- If you want innovation, create happy employees by encouraging their ideas.

Wouldn't this be valuable information to have before you begin working at a new company? It's always better to prevent a problem instead of fixing it after the fact. Too many of us get wrapped up in the superficial, financial, and cultural elements of a potential new job (or don't consider the most important factors because we just want to get out of a really bad job) that we forget what truly motivates us when it comes time to landing a new position. Wouldn't you want to know going in if you will have the freedom to speak your mind and share your ideas?

Remember, the biggest predictor of job satisfaction is the relationship you have with your immediate manager. With that in mind, I came up with one question everyone should ask during the interview process to gain insight into what their manager will be like before they even accept a new job:

"Do you champion new ideas from your team?"

The answer will tell you if the manager wants you just to do what you're told, or if your best ideas can move up the food chain. The answer might surprise you.

I gave this advice to a friend who was miserable in her current job because of a micromanaging boss who didn't value her ideas and she was considering her options. At the time, she was very excited about a new opportunity at a start-up. On the surface, the start-up appeared to be mutually excited that she was joining. The people she met from the company said all the right things about cultural fit and how they would change the world. Still, she felt that something was off.

When she spoke to the hiring manager, she asked the crucial question, "Do you champion new ideas from your team?" The manager seemed uncomfortable but still said, "We are always open to new ideas."

Not many of us want to be handed a series of tasks and told to meet milestones. We'd prefer to fight for our ideas alongside other people in the organization while having the freedom to get ahead and get results but very few of us feel like we have that freedom. If we were to ask our employees the same question, we might be surprised to hear them say how little they feel open to express ideas to their bosses.

My friend did not take that job. All of the people she interviewed left the start-up not long after she interviewed there. And the company went out of business nearly a year after she decided not to join.

Sometimes all we need to do to inspire change is ask this question. That is what happened when I was brought on to work with a major consumer brand during a time when they were experiencing a lot of disruption. I started with 300 employees from one department and asked them this one question at four different times over a year. What I found was that during that year, there was a 20-point increase in employee engagement, and all I had done was conduct that one-question survey.

THE 1-QUESTION SURVEY

ON A SCALE OF 0-10, HOW LIKELY IS YOUR MANAGER TO CHAMPION YOUR IDEAS?

0	1	2	3	4	5	6	7	8	9	10

NOT AT ALL LIKELY   EXTREMELY LIKELY

Simply asking the question encouraged employees to share ideas. It sent the message that employee ideas mattered, and the employees got it without any training from me. They just heard me say that it's important to see management encouraging employee ideas, not just listening to them but supporting their ideas and allowing those ideas to rise up through the organization.

The one-question survey is not only a valuable tool for a prospective employee during the interview process, but it's also a way to define the Champion Leaders who already exist inside the organization. The answer to that one question can reveal much about a company culture. It may prompt more questions to consider.

Are employees likely to express their good ideas? If they do, what happens then? Does the company let good ideas die because its leaders aren't listening? Why is this so common among businesses today? How does this happen?

An even better question: What do you do if you aren't able to turn things around with a bad boss and despite your best efforts, there is no saving the situation? There's an old joke in the industry about when you get stuck with a bad manager, the best thing you can do is leave. Unfortunately, there is some truth to that. Experience has taught me that sometimes we reach a point where it is just time to leave. Life's too short to be miserable with a mean boss, at a mean company, with customers who are miserable, too. Because that just sucks! But you don't want to jump the gun either. Make sure you've given your existing manager the chance to answer the one-question survey before you exit. Give him or her the chance to change. Give them this book!

DON'T BE A MANAGER WHO SUCKS

In his book, *Good to Great: Why Some Companies Make the Leap…and Others Don't,* Jim Collins profiles what he calls Level 5 leaders (William Collins, 2001). Level 5 leaders combine the counterintuitive traits of competence and humility. Specifically, Jim profiles Darwin Smith, who was an extremely successful 20-year CEO of paper company Kimberly-Clark. Most people have likely never heard of Darwin Smith because he was so extremely humble as a leader. He saw his job as serving employees and customers. He was motivated by the feeling that he needed to earn the right to be called CEO every day.

In each of my manager roles, I have tried to embody these ideals. I find that happy people are more productive. Life's too short to be miserable at work, to deal with a manager who sucks, to have prescheduled one-on-ones, and to sit through annual performance reviews. Instead, I would check in with my team about once a week with three questions:

- How are you doing?
- How am I doing?
- How can I help? (This is where I'd champion their ideas.)

That's all you need to know to become your own Champion Leader, but that's only the first step. If you are a Champion Leader, or lucky enough to work for a company and a boss who champions your ideas and puts the customer at the center of the Bullseye, that certainly doesn't mean you're home free. Reaching this point comes with a whole new set of problems that I will address next.

WHAT YOU NEED TO KNOW!

Championing employee ideas creates more job appreciation among employees while fostering an environment of
creativity.

Leaders not only have to champion employee ideas, but
they need to take those ideas seriously to truly activate
their employees.

Champion Leaders who activate their employees by championing their ideas will create an environment better suited
to foster innovation.

Champion Leaders help employees find purpose in their
work.

If you take care of your employees, your employees will take
care of your customers.

Consider utilizing the one-question survey with your employees or during your next job interview by asking, "Do you
champion new ideas from your team?"

Chapter 4:
OUR CUSTOMERS
KNOW WE SUCK

May 12 is a very special day for my family. It was on that day in 2003 that my wife, Liz, gave birth to our oldest daughter, the first of our four children. I can say without a doubt that my kids are the greatest "content" that I've ever created in my life.

In 2018, we hosted a party for our daughter's 15th birthday. After all the guests had left and we had finished cleaning up the house, I checked my email. I saw an email from LinkedIn with a message that read, "Hey everybody, we're celebrating LinkedIn's 15th anniversary. Share pictures to show us what you were doing 15 years ago." My wife and I had to laugh because that brought back a lot of memories from what she was doing 15 years before.

We didn't share pictures of what she was doing then but it did get me thinking. I couldn't believe LinkedIn was only 15 years old. I imagined how much they had changed the world of business and marketing, and I thought about how much my daughter, and having kids in general, had changed my life!

If my daughter shared a birthday with LinkedIn, one of the world's first commercially viable social media networks, what did my other children have in common with this new digital world?

Before closing my laptop, I did a little more digging and found that my second daughter was born about three weeks before the global launch of Facebook, the first Facebook ad, and the founding of Twitter—all in 2006. My oldest son, our third child, was born in 2007 within three weeks of the launch of the iPhone in the United States, and my youngest son was born close to the founding of Snapchat in 2011.

My kids in 2018.

I could see the age of all those digital, social, and mobile technologies on the young faces of my beautiful children. That hammered the point home for me how young those new technologies really are. Fifteen years previously, these companies didn't exist. Fifteen years before that, YouTube didn't exist. My oldest daughter can't legally drive a car; we don't even let my youngest son cross the street on his own. But in the same amount of time that my kids have been alive, these companies have changed our world. The global rate of disruption and change is all happening much faster than we realize.

Also, in the past 15 years, 52 percent of Fortune 500 companies have disappeared from that list. Companies such as American Motors, Brown Shoe, Studebaker, Collins Radio, Detroit Steel, and National Sugar Refining were in the Fortune 500 just 30 years ago but no longer exist. Some of the biggest companies, once the largest and most recognized names in business, are gone. With new players and new technologies entering the marketplace faster than ever, today's companies just aren't around as long. In 2017, 190 of the Fortune 500 had experienced negative growth[xxiv] from lost revenue, lost customers, lost market share, and talent walking out the door.

In 1955, the life expectancy of a company was 75 years. In 2015, it was 15 years; if your company is currently 15 years old, it has already reached its life expectancy. Congratulations if you've made it that far! That's no small feat given that the rate of failure for companies is happening radically faster than it used to.

It's no mystery that emerging digital technologies, and the changes they have brought into the world, are the source of this disruption. The statistics are staggering. As of 2017, Fortune reported that 700 million smartphones were in use worldwide. Facebook has now reached upward of two billion active users. Nearly half of the world's population uses the internet. In a matter of seconds, we can learn the capital of Qatar, find the number of calories in a green pepper, and figure out the time it takes to drive to Albuquerque.

Not only do we now have answers at our fingertips to most imaginable questions, but we're constantly tuned into friends, family, and coworkers through Facebook, Twitter, Instagram, and

LinkedIn. We can better endure a long commute with Spotify, Pandora, or podcasts. We can pass the time during a subway ride by watching a YouTube video or wind down at night with Hulu or Netflix. So much content exists in so many different forms that it's overwhelming and impossible to keep up with everything; our attention is being pulled in a million different directions.

Because these new technologies have changed the way we live our lives and digest content, they can't help but also change the way businesses operate. Companies have many options today for how to convince us to buy their products. They can use Instagram, Snapchat, and Twitter. LinkedIn offers LinkedIn ads, sponsored updates, video ads, and text ads. They can also use Facebook Boost, Facebook Live, podcasts, or animated explainer videos. These technologies and platforms have given companies so many options and opportunities to reach larger audiences that businesses are tempted to try them all! Therefore, they may think that pushing out more promotional material is a good idea so they play the numbers game by trying all the options they have until some of them work.

Once companies exhaust these ideas, they can also advertise with highway billboards or website banner ads. At industry trade shows, their sales and marketing teams hand out pens and stress balls with their company logos to potential customers. These teams will also do their best to land the massive two-story, centrally located booth with amazing LED lighting. This type of all-in marketing strategy is a quick-fix solution for employees looking to show their bosses they've implemented something, but what they've ultimately done is put quantity over quality.

Companies face a challenge: Attention is the new currency. But the harder they try to get that attention, the more they'll see the opposite when audiences eventually tune out. The audience that companies are trying to reach is now so vast and needs to stay engaged. The less that a company provides specific brand engagement for its audience, the less likely the audience is to engage with that brand.

Trying to talk to everyone means we're really talking to no one. All those pop-ups, banner ads, and "buy now" buttons are simply interrupting the way we view content. Understandably, many people think marketing is nothing more than advertising, interruption, and promotion. I'll go so far as to say that the video autoplay pop-up ad is the evilest creation in the history of mankind. Not only are we bored with advertising content but most of us find it incredibly annoying.

THE CUSTOMER JOURNEY

When we need to buy something in our personal lives, we don't call a salesperson. We research it online. Likewise, we don't call a salesperson when we need to buy items for our businesses—we research them online. According to Salesforce.com[xxv], as much as 90 percent of business-purchase research happens before buyers reach out to the vendor they plan to choose.

In some cases, companies are seeing their sales increase by stopping their heavy advertising. According to a recent article in *Ad Age Magazine,* Procter & Gamble, one of the largest advertisers in the world and one of the Fortune 500, did just that. In 2018, it saw its most significant growth in five years, but the kicker is that it wasn't because of advertising. It was because of the complete opposite: Procter & Gamble cut their advertising expenditures[xxvi]. They increased their business by advertising less!

According to the Advertising Research Foundation[xxvii], sales begin to decline after an ad reaches the same person 40 times in a month. In other words, if a company promotes itself twice to the same person on the same day, its sales will go down.

The minute-long ads spliced into the middle of a documentary or the 30-second ads we're required to sit through before watching a video become nothing more than frustrating distractions. The high volume of promotional content that bombards us daily can be exhausting. We certainly don't like it; we may tolerate it but the ads don't engage us. Yet, companies still run lots of those types of ad campaigns.

At least 200 million people worldwide choose to use ad blockers monthly and that number is growing. In other words, 200 million people have taken an extra step and are paying money not to view ads. A 2016 Forbes article reported that 49 percent of online users will ignore brands that push too many ads or show them content that doesn't interest them. This statistic implies that companies investing in heavy-handed, generic, self-promotional content are marketing their products wrong. The same digital marketing strategies that marketers insist will work likely frustrate them when they're the customers.

Consumers do not want to be reminded relentlessly of how great a product is; they'd rather have information that is useful and interesting to them. If marketers considered what does and doesn't make consumers happy, when brainstorming marketing strategies they might change the content they put out into the world. But somewhere along the line, they either stopped caring or convinced themselves these heavy-handed tactics work.

We know that relentless advertising and self-promotion doesn't work. How, then, do brands get through to their potential customers? How can companies expect their content to compete with videos like the one of a cat in a shark costume riding a robotic vacuum while chasing a duck?

Customer journeys are changing for all of us. Regardless of our jobs, these changes will impact what we do and how we do it. Taking the first step on the road to empathy and sucking less means realizing that we just aren't as interesting or as important to other people as we think we are.

Google executive Noah Fenn once said that businesses seem to have "collective amnesia[xxviii]" when they come up with ways to connect with customers. Not only does this thinking change marketing but it changes the infrastructure of some of the biggest businesses in the world.

Let's consider Coca-Cola, arguably one of the world's most recognized brands. When their CMO left a few years ago, the company decided to eliminate the position. Incredibly, one of the world's most successful and famous brands ever decided not to replace their CMO with a marketer. Instead, it appointed a sales executive to the title of "Chief Growth Officer" and made that position responsible for marketing.

When asked about how he would handle the marketing function, the Chief Growth Officer had said, "If you want people to love to drink Coca-Cola, we need to show ads of people who love drinking Coca-Cola[xxix]." Does that sound like something that would make you want to drink more sweet, brown-colored carbonated water? Does that sound like a company that cares about customers? Or its larger purpose? Or its impact on the world?

DO PEOPLE EVEN CARE
ABOUT BRANDS ANYMORE?

A small portion of brands is outperforming their peers, growing their businesses, and at least trying to help the world in their own way by presenting customers with a purpose-driven message. According to the latest research from one of the largest ad agencies in the world[xxx], these "meaningful brands" outperform others by more than 200 percent. What accounts for such a big performance gap in these brand results?

The combination of having a core mission, executing that mission, and messaging makes certain brands more meaningful than others. Some companies may promote an ideal and say they take a customer-centric approach but something completely different happens behind closed doors. When customers learn about these disconnects, the brands will suffer. The brands that really shine through are those that remain consistent in their mission and execution.

Meaningful brands bring the internal culture of empathy full circle. As we start to focus more on our customers, better serve our employees, create goals that make a real impact, and convince our bosses that empathy is a tool to grow business, our workplace culture inevitably changes. That culture change traces back to the customer experience because of the way our customers (and potential customers) see how the company treats those it serves. This will heavily influence the public opinion of a brand.

Plenty of examples come to mind of what we might call a meaningful brand, such as Patagonia, Dove, or Nike. It varies and it needs to be meaningful for each of us. While all meaningful brands stand for something and promote the values that their customers connect with, what sets great branding apart is the fact that it taps into people's emotions, whether those people are customers or not. The brand doesn't reach just the people who buy the product, it also leaves an impression on those who don't. Getting to that point requires asking three very important questions:

• How can we accomplish a deeper connection with consumers through our own branding?

• How can we reach new audiences more effectively by connecting to their values?

• What does it mean to create a meaningful brand experience for our customer?

Brands that promote their values and beliefs will naturally attract customers with similar goals and values—for better or worse—because, as consumers, that's exactly what we look for in businesses. We want to invest in brands that we feel connected to, that feel personal to us, that care about our input and what we stand for. By sticking to their values, regardless of mass appeal, meaningful brands develop genuine customer loyalty. These brands make us feel individually picked out, even if we're one of many. However, not every company is Patagonia. Very few companies can claim to have the same level of brand recognition and loyalty as that. This brand is one of the exceptions and not the rule.

The meaningful brand research study also revealed that 77 percent of us wouldn't care if the products we regularly use were to disappear completely. We see the majority of our products as basically replaceable. We wouldn't care if they were no longer available, mainly because we know that if one brand disappears, there will be another one that can provide us the same product. Whether you are a start-up founder, a senior executive, a marketer, or in any other position in a business, the bottom line is that your customers don't really care about your company as much as you think they do.

Tina Sharkey capitalized on this way of thinking when she started her own company. Before she did that, she was the head of marketing for QVC, the cofounder of iVillage, the head of digital for Sesame Street, and the chairman of BabyCenter. Eventually, she cofounded the company Brandless.

For those of you who have taken your kids to the grocery store, you know it's not a fun experience. Tina had kids too, so she understood the struggle. Tina started Brandless because she believed the in-store shopping experience was less than ideal, even if you don't have little ones asking for candy. She knew how little we trust the brands we use. The idea behind the company is that it sells brandless products—just high-quality items, each for only three dollars. Instead of offering a dozen different hand creams, for example, Brandless offers one, a very good organic one. Each of its product labels reads, "Just what matters."

Arguably, what's most interesting about the company is their corporate mission: "People over brand." Brandless accomplishes this by listening to its customers and creating a two-way conversation to build relationships. As an added touch, Brandless employees handwrite thank-you notes to their customers.

Tina understands that people want to do business with companies that share their values. Accordingly, she roots the company in truth, trust, transparency, and community-driven values. For example, it participates in acts of kindness, such as donating a meal at checkout in the customer's honor. These personalized touches are why Fast Company ranked Brandless as one of the 10 most innovative retail companies in 2018 and 2019[xxxi].

We can all learn from a company like Brandless. Think of how you can put people over brand, customers over products, and employee experiences over org charts. Unfortunately, few companies think like that. Since the very meaning of what it means to be a brand has dramatically changed in a relatively short period of time, how do you stay engaged with a company that isn't as important as it wants to think it is?

WHAT YOU NEED TO KNOW!

Digital and social media technologies are not only changing the way we interact with each other, but they are disrupting the way we do business. The life expectancy of companies has decreased.

We are bombarded with content. We have more options than ever, so businesses are in a cutthroat competition for your attention. Attention is the new currency.

Customers have developed a distrust of brands, and most wouldn't care if many of the brands they use disappear tomorrow.

The bottom line: Customers don't care about your company as much as you think they do.

"No man is an island..."
~ John Donne

Chapter 5:
DON'T SUCK

What do customers care about? What really matters to people these days?

You should be able to answer this one yourself. We're all customers. And if you're reading this book, you either run your own business or work as an employee in a business that needs customers. Maybe you're in a front-line role like marketing, sales, or customer service that deals with customers directly. Or perhaps you're in a support role. No matter what we do, every business needs customers. And every business needs to answer the question, "What do customers want?"

This question is difficult to answer because we have been hardwired to think of customers as percentages, statistics, and an abstract group of demographics. It can be challenging to see our customers as individual people with individual needs and wants. But if we don't know what customers want on a personal level, then how can we deliver what they need?

Let's imagine for a moment you're trying to develop a new product for your business but you haven't yet gathered any demographics on the typical person you want to be the target audience for this product. The average customer could be a 32-year-old single guy living in South Beach or a 70-year-old woman hailing from

Salt Lake City. How could you determine what that customer is looking for in a product?

It's next to impossible to relate to a person you know nothing about. It's even more challenging to get them to buy something from you.

"I KNOW THAT I KNOW NOTHING"

To truly understand people, let's take a step back and admit that we don't know them. "I know that I know nothing," the Socratic paradox by Plato applies here because admitting we don't have all the answers leaves us open to learning. An openness to learning gives us an immediate advantage over all the bosses and executives who are convinced they already know it all. Had it not been for my first job in sales, I might not have been as receptive to this idea.

After college, I started working at Nielsen, the TV ratings company, in a division called retail measurement. What Nielsen did, and still does to this day, is track all the product sales at a store. It then packages that data and sells it back to the retailers and manufacturers to provide them with what we call in marketing the Four Ps: Which products you're selling at what price in which place and on what level of promotion. One of the most important lessons I learned working that job was that every company thinks they know things they actually don't know.

My first client was the Sargento cheese company. It is now one of the most recognized cheese brands in the US, but at the time, they were a growing cheese company based in Plymouth, Wisconsin. Their product was mostly distributed throughout the Midwest and they wanted to expand. My client contact was a man named Barry. I was just starting my career and was full of enthusiasm, and Barry was at the other end of his career. When I tried to sell him our products, he wasn't all that interested.

This was in 1994, when having email and desk computers was still new, and it turned out that Barry didn't know how to use his computer. One day when I showed up at his office, he asked me to help him with it. I had given up on trying to sell Barry anything, but once I helped him with his computer, we started talking. Suddenly, he started to open up in ways that he never had during my initial sales pitches.

I learned from Barry that the Sargento company thought it was selling its products in many cities. Then, I showed him my data. The research proved that what he thought he knew, and what others had told him, simply wasn't true. He needed the hard data to show his sales team; retailers in more cities had said they would sell Sargento products but the team hadn't followed through.

Showing Barry what he didn't know was how I sold him a deeper set of data. In my first year working with my new friend Barry, I had more than doubled our sales. But Barry's situation wasn't unique. I had countless conversations with executives that followed that same pattern. I'd always start with the same pitch: "Hey, we've got data and insights that can help improve your sales."

"Nah, we already know that."

Then I would show them the data, and they'd be surprised that they didn't know such crucial business details as products sold and at what price. These situations taught me how big the disconnect really was between the company and its customers.

Have you ever watched a commercial and thought to yourself:

Who approved that? How did this commercial get made? These days it seems like more than half the commercials we watch fit into that category. Generally, it's because of an executive who didn't understand the target audience and thought that he or she knew better. As I've said before, behind every bad idea is an executive who asked for it. That executive didn't want to learn, was not open to outside opinion, and felt that he or she knew best.

True wisdom is knowing what we don't know. We'll never be open to other possibilities if we don't accept that we don't know everything.

WHO KNOWS YOUR CUSTOMER BEST?

You may not know every customer best but someone in your company will. In any organization, the people who understand the customer best are those who work most closely with them. These jobs aren't always the most glamorous ones or the ones we immediately point to when we think of what's most important in the overall operation but they make the most significant impact on the customer's experience. They're up close and personal.

Who do you think is the most important person working at a hospital? Many people will say the doctors. The doctors have the highest degrees, they diagnose patients, and they perform surgery. The doctors are certainly important; a hospital couldn't function without them.

But when we change the question to focus on the patient's point of view, we change the answer. Most patients will probably say that nurses have the most important job in a healthcare setting. It's the nurses who spend the most time with patients. Patients highly value the comfort and advice that nurses provide because nurses often know the patients better than the doctors do.

Patients staying in the hospital for extended periods may bond with the nurses who get to know their personalities and idiosyncrasies. For example, nurses become familiar with their patients' eating and sleeping habits. And because the nurses are directly involved with the most personal aspects of a hospital stay, they see a patient's most vulnerable moments.

When a hospital wants to develop a better patient experience, who do you think they should start with? Ensuring that patients are happy requires hospitals to listen to the nurses because they have their fingers on the pulse of what's happening on the ground. The lesson to be learned: we need to empower those who have the highest customer experience knowledge.

EVEN I SUCK SOMETIMES!

For the first 10 years of my marriage, I tried so hard to be a good husband by surprising my wife with romantic gifts for birthdays and holidays. But every single time, I failed to get her what she really wanted. When I realized I couldn't do it alone, I turned for advice to those closest to my wife—her mother and her sisters— but that didn't work either.

Since then, I've learned to take a different approach. I still want to surprise her, she still wants to be surprised, but she also wants what she wants. Now, I ask her to give me a list of three or five different things she would definitely want, and then I try to surprise her by picking out one of the five. She likes to keep me guessing, but I'm sure she would say that these past 10 years have been much better on the gift-giving front.

Often our initial instincts are wrong and what we think people want isn't always the case. The result of most marketing tests I've conducted, even something as simple as making the "buy now" button red or green, is almost always the opposite of what my team initially thought. What we may think will work often doesn't. That's why thinking we know everything is so dangerous—and why there are so many bad commercials out there. The answer to the problem could be simple, so we should just ask!

The first thing I do with my clients during workshops is to ask them, "If you could ask your customers one question, what would it be?" The right question to ask them would be "What's your biggest challenge?" or something similar around their personal concerns. When businesses really understand the biggest challenges and concerns of the audience they're trying to reach, they are better equipped to solve that problem, quell that concern, and answer that question. However, few companies take the time to ask.

We don't need to be totally reliant on the customer for answers. We can figure out a lot on our own if we know where and how to look. Sarah Minella Sugarman is the Senior Manager of Marketing Communications for a Global Imaging Company. Sarah and her team asked me to help them create content to engage with radiologists. To find out the concerns that radiologists may have, we typed "radiologist" into a search engine to see what came up in the autofill.

When we type any word into a search engine, autofill will complete it based on the volume of searches. In other words, it will tell us the questions people are asking, and those questions almost always come down to life, love, money, and their various pursuits of happiness. For example, when we read those articles or lists about the most searched-for beer or most used adjectives in each state, they're basically using autofill to determine search histories.

From our search, we learned radiologists were mostly concerned about salary. In addition to showing some of their questions about the necessary education and best location for their industry, the autofill feature also revealed that radiologists were often stressed, overworked, and worried that they were being replaced by artificial intelligence (AI). In less than one minute, we were able to learn so much more about the needs and concerns of radiologists because of autofill.

First after our research, we created a "Radiologist's Salary Guide." Next, we wrote articles on how radiologists could better cope with workplace stress. Finally, we detailed the opportunities and impact of AI on the field of radiology. In other words, we let radiologists tell us what they were searching for, and then we set out to create that content for them.

The first couple of articles published on the client's website had 10 times more traffic than its average content. Today, our efforts with this company continue to produce subscribers to its site and leads for its sales team that it had never had before. Once we knew what our customers were asking and what their biggest challenges were, we could then take the next step of providing the answers.

ANSWER THE QUESTIONS
CUSTOMERS ARE ASKING

My friend Jason Miller used to be the Head of Content and Social Media at Marketo and LinkedIn, and he now works as the

Head of Brand Marketing at Microsoft. Unbelievably, Jason has a passion for B2B marketing. What's impressive is how he has found a way to marry that with his passion for rock and roll—not just any rock and roll but 1980s hair metal. He has written a best-selling marketing book called *Welcome to the Funnel* (Heavy Metal Thunder, 2014), a book about B2B demand generation with a title that's a wordplay on the Guns N' Roses song and released a photo collection of his pictures taken at hair metal concerts over the years.

When he took the job at LinkedIn, Jason wanted to inspire the organization to think of every job as a customer service job. LinkedIn sells many different products—HR solutions, marketing solutions, sales solutions, and a training platform to support all that. Jason wanted to find a way that the employees could tap into their passions while serving their customers. How could he inspire those in the organization to do that?

First, he asked, "What are the questions our customers are looking to get answered?" He figured out the different interests that people had and also the content customers were reading and sharing. He identified the questions his audience had based on the keywords they used.

Next, he started answering those questions with his own content. He wrote articles such as "5 Tech Companies Killing It with Content on LinkedIn" and "How to Deal with a Narcissist at Work—And Why You Need To." He also wrote blog posts and created a sophisticated marketers podcast with useful content for his target audience. All of his content aimed simply to answer the questions his customers were asking.

Jason truly embraced what it meant to be a Champion Leader

when realizing that he couldn't do this all on his own. More importantly, he realized that he wasn't utilizing all available resources within the company. To truly focus on the customer, he would need to involve everyone around him.

Jason tapped into some of LinkedIn's research and learned that 3 percent of employees at the average company were driving 30 percent of the clicks on corporate content. He realized employees could be the key to storytelling success if he were able to activate their passions and expertise and encourage them to collaborate across the organization to deliver results. He understood that employees have 10 times as many social media connections as corporate social media accounts. Employees represent a massive opportunity that many companies are barely tapping into.

Jason recognized that he worked with many smart marketing, sales, and HR people at LinkedIn. He wanted them to tell their stories, but when he reached out and asked them, he found his colleagues were reluctant to share them. He thought about paying them for their contributions, but he didn't have the budget and that just didn't seem authentic.

He realized that we can't make people care about the content, the customers, or even the companies they work for. If we can't make people care, how can we convince them to contribute? The answer was simple: Tell them what's in it for them. He promised three things that would encourage and incentivize his employees to contribute content that they already knew and loved:

1. You can build your own personal connections.

2. You can build your personal brand.

3. You can propel your career at LinkedIn or elsewhere.

Jason led by example. First, he started writing content twice a month. Next, he created a sales deck and pitched his concept to sales, HR, and all the different departments in LinkedIn. He asked employees to share their passions and expertise with the world so they could make an impact, but this time he showed them what was in it for them. He wasn't asking them to do it for him; he wanted them to do it because it would benefit them in the long run. This convinced his colleagues to follow his example.

One of those colleagues was Sean Callahan. It turns out Sean had a background as a newspaper and magazine reporter before he joined LinkedIn in 2014. Sean was put on Jason's team. He told me that they "liked each other almost immediately. I've never met anyone quite like Jason. He's a complete original."

Jason recruited Sean to work with another teammate, Alex Rynne, to start contributing to the LinkedIn marketing blog. And Sean and Alex started creating useful content to help marketers on a regular basis. They are both still contributing members of that team, having won numerous awards and recognition for their writing contributions.

After one year, Jason and his colleagues, Sean and Alex, had reached millions of people with their content, which got more than 100,000 clicks combined. Just these three employees publishing three to six posts a month were able to generate millions of impressions and more than 100,000 clicks. If they had paid to get that much traffic to their content, it would have cost hundreds of thousands of dollars! Further, that engagement and those clicks that were generated without any budget provided leads for sales that they could measure.

Jason saw that employees were the key to sales, marketing, and HR success. He activated the passion and expertise of those employees by showing them what was in it for them and having them focus on what they already knew and loved.

Don't underestimate the potential impact and social media influence of your fellow employees. Your creatives, data analysts, strategists, and other experts on your team are the skilled, passionate, and knowledgeable influencers people want to learn from. Here are some ideas we can learn from Jason's example:

- Who in your organization has the desire to share news, insights, and their own thoughts on social media profiles and other available outlets?

- Who on your team is a financial or data expert and what financial advice can your experts share by writing featured blog posts on your company website?

- Are there engineers and technical people on your team who are interested in sharing their knowledge through online tutorials, Q&A sessions, and live streaming?

- Can you harness customers and influencers through authentic content and stories where they have some of the creative control?

All of this can become premium content that stirs up interest while building relationships between your customers and your experts. By building up your employees' online presence on LinkedIn, you give them name recognition as an expert, and you get even more influence with your audience.

Your company should consider how expensive new customers are to convert compared to the ROI generated by your existing customers. Studies show that it costs five to seven times more to acquire a new customer than it does to motivate action from a current customer. What better way to attract new customers than by using company experts to generate content that answers their questions? Companies with engaged employees outperform those without engaged employees by as much as 202 percent, according to Gallup, so companies benefit when they pay attention to their employees.

Your company doesn't have a face, a soul, or a heartbeat. It's a thing. It doesn't have a family. It doesn't struggle or accomplish anything on its own. How can you really expect your customers to trust it? People, on the other hand, can provide that personal touch by empathizing with the customer. When your employees become the face of your company, you're giving the customer someone to believe in. That's powerful stuff! Your company should talk with your fellow employees and ask what support they need to create a platform to share their expertise.

WHAT YOU NEED TO KNOW!

You will never be able to reach your customers as long as you think of them as statistics and not people.

Admit that you don't know what you don't know, because it will allow you to learn.

Find the people in your organization who know the customer best and listen to what they have to say.

Ask! When you don't know, ask.

Find out what questions your customers are asking and set out to answer those questions.

Nobody does it alone. Call upon your co-workers and employees to help reach your customers and answer the questions they are asking.

Chapter 6:
EMPATHY WINS

We've learned the importance of what we do: Engaging employees, championing their ideas, putting customers at the center of the Bullseye, and answering the questions they ask. But what you're doing isn't the only important aspect. How you do it will ultimately determine your effectiveness. This is where empathy comes in.

In today's world, empathy is an important sentiment that often gets lost in the chaos. We've forgotten what it really means to genuinely connect with someone, which is unfortunate because everything in our lives boils down to relationships. We may have close relationships with our partners, siblings, and longtime friends that play vital roles in our personal and social lives. Other encounters, however insignificant, can constitute different types of relationships.

Those smaller interactions — like those with our colleagues or customers — shape our life experiences more indirectly but also affect our perception of the world. When we engage with the world, our experiences rest on our communication and interaction with others. Empathy is what makes that communication and that interaction run as smoothly as possible.

Empathy is defined by the dictionary as "the action of understanding, being aware of, being sensitive to, and vicariously experiencing the feelings, thoughts, and experience of another of either the past or present without having the feelings, thoughts, and experience fully communicated in an objectively explicit manner."

Empathy is about walking in our neighbors' shoes, even for just a little while. Empathy gives us the ability to understand what others are experiencing either because we've gone through a similar experience ourselves or because we can imagine enough how we'd feel if we were going through it. It's why we say, "I've been there" when someone we know is going through a tough time. It's the reason we can seem to feel the actual emotions when someone we know is struggling. It's why we get that little lump in our throats during movies when a loveable character dies in a tragic battle scene or finds out the person they love doesn't return the feeling.

One of my former colleagues could not watch violent movies or TV shows because she claimed that she could actually feel the pain she was watching. She even pointed me to research that showed that a small number of people can actually experience the same emotions that others go through when they watch TV shows, commercials, or movies. They feel the exact sensations they're watching — even physical pain and suffering — which understandably makes fight scenes in movies impossible to watch. We understand what it feels like, or what it would feel like, to be in their shoes. Empathy is an integral part of the human condition.

Understanding the experiences that others are going through hasn't always been about crying over our popcorn at the movies. Empathy bands us together. It's served us in fight-or-flight scenarios throughout human evolution. According to an article published in *Psychology Today*, the empathy trait has strengthened and developed over time[xxxii].

Millions of years ago, in the era of our ancestors, having a deeper connection with the people within one's group became a component of connection to the group. Through time, empathy has developed into a crucial part of everything we do, from winning a playoff game on a team you love to staying alive in a community you were born into. Researchers hypothesize that this happened for many reasons, but two stand out.

1. We needed to empathize with our offspring.

To keep our lineage thriving, we needed to nurture our children, want the best for them, and put their interests above our own. This can feel challenging when it happens to us. For example, there is a reason the sound of a newborn baby crying will wake us from a dead sleep or annoy us like nothing else on a crowded flight.

2. We simply did better as a species when we lived and operated as a group.

We have descended from humans who were more likely to nurture tribal relationships, work together, and contribute different skills and talents to the collective. Working together wasn't just more effective, it was ultimately safer. Empathy was baked into our evolution over time, and it's allowed us to continue working in productive teams in the various facets of our lives. As the saying goes: There's power in numbers. The benefits of forming a culture of empathy hold true in the modern world.

Empathy is essential in grabbing, and keeping, the attention of others, specifically our customers. We want our products to feel relatable and necessary. To know what that means, we need to know them, to put ourselves in their shoes. It keeps us working as a team on our goals as a business. It further connects coworkers and employees with their managers and each other.

A culture of empathy that pervades a business has a direct economic value, too. Empathy in the workplace has been shown to drive actual business results through its many ripple effects. It promotes a positive work environment, which means less turnover and increased productivity among employees, leading to a better product for the customer. It can transform a business' profitability and internal cost level.

Though challenging, empathy within organizations truly bridges the gap between what your executives expect, what our colleagues expect, and what our customers look for. We just need the know-how to tap into it. We must forget about our traditional business instinct and focus on that sweet spot in the middle—the overlap between what we want, what customers might want, and what our fellow employees want.

THE CLEVELAND CLINIC EMPATHY SERIES

My friend, Amanda Todorovich, is the Senior Director of Content at Cleveland Clinic. Amanda lives in Cleveland. She and her family were patients of Cleveland Clinic, and Amanda had always enjoyed her experience with the hospital system.

Cleveland Clinic has long been dedicated to putting "Patients First." It's not only based in Cleveland, Ohio, it operates all over the world. It calls all its employees "caregivers." When Amanda first arrived at Cleveland Clinic, its leadership wanted to take it one step further and encourage its 40,000+ employees to utilize the power of empathy. So, its Patient Experience Office and in-house media production team created a video called "Empathy: The Human Connection to Patient Care." This three-minute video wasn't really ever intended to be seen by an outside audience. (Look it up. It might make you cry.)

It had a simple premise:

"If you could stand in someone else's shoes, would you treat them differently?"

The video included a series of vignettes that exemplify the pain, struggle, and happy times that unfold inside a hospital system.

We meet one fearful older gentleman who has been dreading his appointment and worries he waited too long.

We meet a desperate family whose 19-year-old son is on life support.

We meet a woman who had a heart transplant 29 days earlier.

We meet a woman who received a terrible diagnosis and is too shocked to comprehend the treatment options ahead of her.

We meet a young girl who is petting a dog for comfort because she is visiting her dad for the last time. (Grab the tissues!)

It's hard not to watch these stories and get choked up. I've seen that video 50 times and I still get chills. We can all see ourselves in those situations, and unfortunately maybe some of you have been in similar situations. The video is powerful and that's why it works.

This video captured the power of empathy for Cleveland Clinic's leadership. It demonstrated that if you stand in someone else's shoes, you will treat them differently. The video harnessed the true power of Cleveland Clinic's brand: We have empathy. We treat each patient as they should be treated.

What Amanda's team soon realized was that this message was one too good to be kept under wraps. They decided to give it the "full-blown social media treatment." It was posted on Facebook, Twitter, YouTube, and its consumer blog, Health Essentials (then known as HealthHub).

Unexpectedly, the tear-jerker went viral. It was recirculated in healthcare circles and now has over four million views on YouTube alone.

Knowing what resonates with patients is what Amanda has built her success on at Cleveland Clinic, leading her to be named Content Marketer of the Year by the Content Marketing Institute in 2016.

It's the story behind the award-winning site Health Essentials, which aims to develop hyper-relevant content to address the health concerns of the more than six million people who visit it each month.

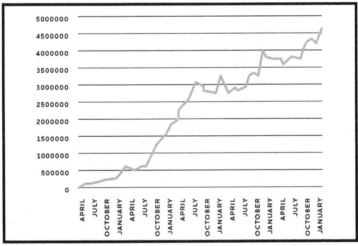

Source: Amanda Todorovich on ContentMarketingInstitute.com

It started out as a fledgling site back in 2012 but is now the most visited hospital blog in the nation, going from zero to 67 million sessions in just six years.

They cover everything from diet to heart disease. There is an entire article about bacon. Who doesn't love bacon? Have you ever wondered if being "sleep drunk" is actually a thing? Well, a new study reveals that it's quite common. I know that because I read the article. Suffering from a broken heart is a real syndrome called, yes, "broken heart syndrome," and it can feel like a heart attack. I know because there's a video about it.

They even set out to answer the question on the minds of everyone: "What does the color of your urine say about you?" Amanda says they (seriously!) looked hard at data to decide whether to use the word "pee" or "urine" on the actual infographic. (I'm not making this up. She said this on a stage in front of hundreds of people at a conference I attended.) Their data analysis revealed that "urine" worked in the article title, but "pee" resonated more with the average person in the image.

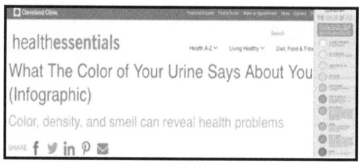

Source: ClevelandClinic.com

Why has Cleveland Clinic's content strategy worked? It's because Amanda's team successfully builds on producing the right content, putting it in front of the right audience, and being useful, helpful, and relevant to people in a way that's unique to Cleveland Clinic.

Its editorial team publishes only three to five articles a day, but they have articles with as many as 65,000 social shares. Your entire website might not get 65,000 social shares. That's well above the average, and Amanda's team has dozens more articles with tens of thousands of shares.

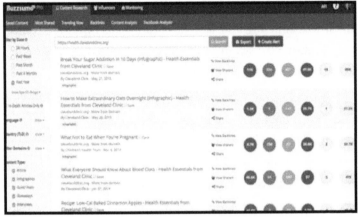

Source: Buzzsumo.com

Amanda and Cleveland Clinic are creating content that competes with cat videos. (I mean, there's always a place for those, right?!) It provides content that its readers need for themselves — and their families — many times, when they need it most.

The key to being successful is knowing your audience and what your audience needs — whether that's how to treat their diabetes, lose weight, or manage their pain. Another lesson learned? You can't start with the results desired. Rather, you have to start with why it's important. Cleveland Clinic's editorial team puts the patient at the center of what they do and uses its content to reach more and more lives every day. This approach delivers more ROI than any ad ever could!

Cleveland Clinic Health Essentials gets so much traffic that Amanda decided to monetize the site in 2015. Why would one of the largest and most respected nonprofit hospitals in the country want to do this? It's just as the advertising policy at the bottom of its ads explains: It's to support its mission — to provide better care of the sick, investigation into their problems, and further education to those they serve (whether they're patients or not!).

According to Amanda, the ads generate revenue that covers the cost of their content operation and more. It's turned into a profit center for the organization.

What Cleveland Clinic's amazing story teaches us is that *empathy is the counterintuitive secret to success.* Cleveland Clinic could have hired an agency and spent lots of money on creative ads that talked about how awesome it is.

But at the end of the day, Cleveland Clinic has created (and continues to create) content that is empathetic. After all, empathy is the ability to understand and share the feelings of another. That's what's behind every story Amanda's team tells.

The lesson of empathy is true for business and it's also true for life. **When we put others ahead of ourselves, we can achieve more success for ourselves.**

When looking at Amanda's story, it forces us to think really hard about how businesses operate and the role that empathy can play.

WHAT YOU NEED TO KNOW!

Empathy evolved in humans because it increased our chances of survival.

Stories based on empathy have the power to move people to action.

Businesses who employ empathy can achieve higher profits and bigger growth.

It may seem counterintuitive, but when we put others ahead of ourselves, we can actually achieve more success.

Chapter 7:
TELL THE STORY

In their bestselling book, *Made to Stick: Why Some Ideas Survive, and Others Die* (Penguin Random House, 2007), Chip and Dan Heath discuss a study conducted in 2004 by researchers at Carnegie Mellon University that illustrates one of the recognizable downsides to our empathetic wiring. They studied participants who received two different kinds of donation requests from the well-known nonprofit Save the Children, an organization that aims to promote all children's rights and provide support around the globe to uphold them.

The first request used a number-heavy approach: "Donate $25 and feed a child for a month. Just under a dollar a day will feed this starving child." The second took a more narrative, storytelling approach where they profiled the children and told the story of their suffering. The participants who were told the personal story gave more than double the amount of those who read the number-heavy request. Why wouldn't both letters warrant the same donation? Better yet: why wouldn't the request that described the sheer number of people going hungry or the low cost of feeding them warrant a bigger donation?

The outcome isn't surprising given what we know about our biology and the way empathy affects our thinking. Real stories about real people that help us to actually "feel" for the other person motivate us best to any kind of action.

I like to imagine cavemen sitting around a fire. One of them starts to tell a story about another caveman that they could all relate to. He talks about the funny grunts he makes when he's hungry. He talks about the cavewoman he had a crush on. They all laugh when he tells them about how bad his farts smelled.

And then he tells them about how one day he woke up really hungry. They hadn't had any meat for a while, so he ran out of his cave and saw a bush with berries on it. He describes the bush. He describes where it grew. He describes the color, the texture, and the smell of the berries. He explains how any caveman would think they look delicious. He was so hungry that he grabbed a bunch and ate them quickly. Then the caveman tells them, in gruesome detail, all the horrible things that happened to him. He had eaten poisonous berries. It's a slow and painful death...

The cavemen sitting around that fire used stories not just because they helped to pass the time but because stories conveyed important pieces of information—information that was key to their survival. The best storytellers all have empathy. They know how to make us laugh. They know how to make us feel like we know the hero of the story. Who's the hero of my poison berry story? Everyone sitting around the fire, because they will have learned not to eat the poisonous berries.

What makes storytelling so effective for learning? According to Vanessa Boris in Harvard Business Review[xxxiii], effective storytelling forges bonds between the listeners based on shared ideas. Those shared ideas create the bonds that define our culture, our values, and our shared history. Numbers may provide the most

accurate insights, but sobering statistics and percentages aren't always the best way to show us what's at stake. It's human nature to
feel for others.

So, what does this have to do with mean people? Remember,
empathy is the counterintuitive secret to getting what we want in
life. Our instinct may drive us to say, "Give me berries! I'm hungry!" But the smartest people in the world understand the power
of empathy and how to use it to tell stories that bond people together under common ideas. Through storytelling, we have the
best method for truly getting what we want in life and business.

STORIES INCREASE VALUE

Great leaders use the power of empathy to tell stories that inspire people to achieve common goals. But can we actually put a
value on the increase we could get from telling better stories? Is
there value in becoming a better storyteller?

"STORIES ARE SUCH A POWERFUL DRIVER OF EMOTIONAL VALUE THAT THEIR IMPACT CAN BE MEASURED OBJECTIVELY."

Source: SignificantObjects.com

A couple of years ago I was having coffee with Michele Miller, a local content strategist and self-described storyteller. We were talking about this very question: What is the value of better storytelling? She asked if I had ever heard of Significant Objects. After I replied that I hadn't, she gave me the overview and shared a SlideShare presentation[xxxiv] she had put together. This changed my life.

Rob Walker and Joshua Glenn were reporters, one for *The Washington Post* and the other for *The New York Times.* They considered themselves storytellers who believed in the power of stories to create quantifiable value through empathy. They wanted to test their hypothesis, so they came up with this idea called the Significant Objects Project. They theorized that sincere stories were such a driver of emotional connection that their impact could be measured objectively.

They started by buying 100 useless trinkets at garage sales and online, all for a few dollars each. They then turned to their col-

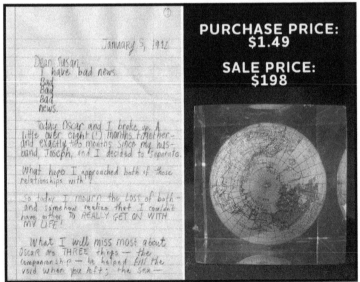

Source: SignificantObjects.com

leagues and a community of writers to provide a backstory for each object. Those writers included bestselling authors, Pulitzer Prize winners, journalists, and mommy bloggers, and they were each asked to write one story about one of the objects.

One writer penned a fictional letter by a woman named Susan about a globe paperweight that Rob and Joshua had purchased for $1.49. In four pages, "Susan" told an elaborate tale of love lost, amazing sex, travel, regret, loneliness, and questions of self-worth. When the letter was attached to that item, the $1.49 globe paperweight sold for $198. That's a 132,000 percent difference!

Rob and Joshua had spent $129 on 100 items purchased in thrift stores, garage sales, and online. Those items then sold for $3,613 online once the fictional stories were added to the items. The final markup average for those 100 items was about 2,700 percent. The point is that *stories have real value.*

THE PIXAR SECRET

Everyone remembers Steve Jobs as the cofounder of Apple, but not everyone remembers his second-greatest accomplishment to the world. In 1985, Jobs bought Pixar from George Lucas for ten million dollars. Pixar released *Toy Story* and a series of movies that were more successful than any movie ever released by a Hollywood studio. Then, in 2006, Jobs sold the company to Disney for seven billion dollars. This increase in value happened because of the company's ability to tell amazing stories consistently.

Clearly, Jobs was on to something, and we saw what happened next when, after teaming with Disney, they created *Frozen,* the

most successful animated film up to that time. It won the Acade-
my Award® for Best Animated Feature Film, and "Let It Go" won
the Oscar® for Best Original Song. However, it almost didn't get
released[xxxv].

When the new boss (Disney) took over, they wanted the film's
story to follow the classic Disney model with princes, princesses,
and castles. That was the initial direction of the story but then they
screened the film about a year into production.

Normally, at an internal screening of a Pixar film, people re-
acted. They laughed out loud. They would bring boxes of tissues
and cry openly. In the end, they would all hug and high-five each
other. But after that first screening of *Frozen*, the employees at
Pixar did not laugh, cry, or high-five. They filed out of the theater
with their unused tissues knowing that this film was going to be
an absolute disaster, Pixar's first flop.

The head writer of the film, along with the songwriters, went to
the producers and asked if they could take over and tell the story they wanted to tell. They reached into their own backgrounds
and the origin of the script. This was not a story about princes
and princesses and ball gowns and castles, although it would have
those elements. It was a story about women and not needing a
man to save them. It was also a story about sisters growing up and
not being "frozen" in the face of fear. They rewrote the script that
ultimately became the version of Disney and Pixar's *Frozen* that
we know today.

It all happened because they made the decision to tell the story that came from within and the one that they felt needed to
be told. They told the story they thought the audience needed
to hear, not the glossy version Disney wanted. *Frozen* was a hit

because we could all see ourselves in the characters struggling to connect with someone they love.

There are different approaches to storytelling, but one of the most well-known was created by Joseph Campbell, who studied 200 memorable stories from every culture around the world in his book, *The Power of Myth* (Anchor Doubleday, 1988). He created what is known as "the hero's journey," which is the common element in all good stories from the beginning of time. It follows this straightforward pattern.

- It starts with a reluctant hero (like Luke Skywalker).

- The hero is called to adventure (to help free Princess Leia).

- He or she goes on a journey far away from home (another planet!).

- On the journey, he or she faces a challenge (learning the ways of the Force) or an obstacle (facing Darth Vader and stopping the evil Empire).

- Our hero overcomes that obstacle (blowing up the Death Star) and transforms (into a Jedi).

- Thus, the hero's journey is resolved.

In the book *Creativity, Inc.,* Pixar's cofounder and former president, Ed Catmull, explains how anyone can scale creativity and achieve the consistent success Pixar did (Random House, 2014). Ed explains how the hero of his story was his team. Pixar had a completely flat structure and a famous vetting process for their story ideas where they would bring in 50 employees from throughout the company to talk about story ideas and plot lines. Anyone could contribute to the conversation and say what they thought.

The hero of Ed's story was his team, and the hero of the team's story was the audience. The audience was the movie watcher they were trying to reach. In other words, "It's not about you!" (That's a famous line from *The Incredibles.*)

Pixar's formula is a variation on Campbell's hero's journey. The Pixar Storytelling Formula is simple:

- Once upon a time…

- Every day…

- One day…

- Because of that…

- Because of that…

- Until finally…

It sounds oversimplified and a little ridiculous written out like that, so we can apply the formula to an enormously successful film like *Finding Nemo* to see it better:

Once upon a time, there was a sad but devoted widowed fish father named Marlin. *And every day* he warned his son, Nemo, of the danger of going out into the open ocean. *One day,* Nemo decided that he would do it anyway, so he swam out into the open water because he was a curious and rebellious kid. *Because of that,* Nemo was kidnapped by a diver. *Because of that,* Marlin traveled the ocean and met his new friend, Dory, *until finally* Marlin and Nemo were reunited.

We're skipping over some important moments in the film, but we can see the formula at work. Every Pixar story follows this formula. In fact, nearly every great story follows some version of this and Joseph Campbell's formula. What's even more interesting is how this formula applies to us and the stories we tell.

How many times do we intuitively jump to the conclusion when we tell people our stories? We can look again at each step of our stories so far. Marlin and Nemo aren't reunited until the very end. "Don't eat poisonous berries" is the last thing we learned in the caveman's story. Luke Skywalker doesn't blow up the Death Star until the very end. We see many steps in each story before the conclusion. About 90 minutes of *Finding Nemo* go by before Marlin finds Nemo. That 90 minutes focuses on the challenges and the problem Marlin was trying to solve, which was finding his son, Nemo.

What does this mean for us? The challenge for us in this fast-paced, digital, text-driven world is to tell stories that show others that we care about them. We can do this by working with our teams to make customers the hero of our story. We can do this by working with leaders across our organizations to make our colleagues the heroes of our stories. We do this by working with our neighbors to support each other in the neighborhood. We do this by starting conversations with our partners that are based on what they want, before we get to the part where we ask for what we want.

My friend, Andrew Davis, explains it like this: think about how we can help to send people we know on a journey they didn't expect to go on, to solve a problem they didn't realize they had, while facing their many demons to overcome the real villain and to emerge as the hero at the end.

I love to point to the Pixar Storytelling Formula because it shows that we are often too quick to jump to solutions in business and in life. Most movies spend that first 90 minutes on the problem and only the last 15 minutes on the resolution. Sometimes, in order to create empathy, we need to marinate in the pain or the challenge others face. We need to make sure everyone feels that pain. It is only then that we can start to set up our audience, and ourselves, for the changes that we need to make in order to transform.

How often do we try to position that solution as us, our products, or our own intelligence? But if we focus the majority of our attention on understanding the problem, the challenge, the dilemma, or the pain that those around us are feeling, we might make a friend for life.

AMBITIOUS STORYTELLING

Whether we are in marketing or not, we can consider how storytelling holds up when compared to the more traditional ways that businesses try to market themselves. We can start by thinking about a typical campaign landing page. Maybe our sales team has an idea for a great campaign, so we have meetings and then more meetings about those meetings. Then we hire an agency and spend a lot more time and money, which leads to many creative ideas and the company spending more money for that landing page. We spend even more money to position and target our audience with this terrific campaign idea. One day the money runs out so the campaign dies. No one ever visited that great landing page we spent so much time and money creating because our ad budget ran out and our idea was never introduced to the world. Even if the campaign did see the light of day, it would still be a one-time, value-based event, if we are lucky.

The big difference between that landing page and a storytelling platform is that storytelling platforms are assets that have real value and grow over time, like a retirement account or an investment account with a compound return. When we publish a consistent amount of content over a period of time, we start to build a community based on those shared ideas. The audience we are engaging increases over time while the investment remains the same. Why does that happen?

The expertise shared in the stories we publish remains relevant a year, two years, and sometimes even three years later. Because the audience increases over time so does any potential revenue we might be able to get from it. That's the power of storytelling for any business versus standard promotion, and it's that increased ROI over time that will have an impact on any CEO.

This was the approach taken by Jill Kouri, whom I met when we were both on the board of a business marketing association. She told me the story of when she was promoted to CMO of Jones, Lang, and LaSalle (JLL), a commercial real estate business based in Chicago. As the new CMO, Jill made it a point to build marketing communications as a strategic function.

Jill redefined what marketing meant for their organization. She focused on building a diverse group of storytellers. In a 2016 interview Jill said, "We are committed to maintaining a culture that unleashes the full potential of all employees. We recognize that diversity is a core component of our business and the right thing to do for our workforce and communities[xxxvi]."

Jill built a team of storytellers, and they started telling more human stories about everything we may need to know in commercial real estate. They strived to help their clients achieve their ambitions, and that stemmed from the belief that every accomplishment begins with a unique ambition. The company launched a new content hub, and they released it in October 2017. It was called *Ambitions,* a magazine and website that became a source for the stories they told about their clients. They took case studies and turned them into human interest stories.

They used multiple platforms to layer their content. After the magazine was released, online videos would be posted on the company website expanding on those stories. They also wanted to use the platform to tell the company's own personal story to help people get to know them. The platform quickly generated interest. They printed 3,000 copies of the first issue and 5,000 with the very next issue. Through it all, Jill and JLL never lost sight of the human element. Because of their amazing platform, JLL was runner-up for the Content Marketer of the Year Award by the Content Marketing Institute in 2018; they won many other awards that proved JLL had become a great place to work.

That story isn't just about marketing. It's about how Jill made her team the hero of her story. She built a team of engaged storytellers and that became a strategic asset across the entire business. Just like Jill, and Jason and Kristen, we can do the same when we remember that we are the hero of this story. Whatever challenges led us to buy this book, we are all on a journey and we are not alone. We can overcome the lack of empathy in our lives, in our work, and in the projects we work on every day. And we can achieve the success we seek.

It starts by taking one step, then one step at a time. We won't allow ourselves to be derailed by the villain of our story, the mean people who suck, or the "friends" who don't care about us. We can emerge as the hero by simply committing to caring a bit more and following the golden rule.

Now maybe you are thinking, *That all sounds great, but what if the villain of my story is the boss who still wants me to do the stuff that doesn't work?* My boss would never let me do something like that! I can relate. I've worked for some of those bosses. The trick is to learn how to push back on doing what most of us are asked to do without upsetting our bosses, as in the "you can have your cake but you can't tell me how to make it" story from Chapter 1. We learn next in Chapter 8 how we can apply this story to our own situation.

WHAT YOU NEED TO KNOW!

Personal stories motivate, inspire, and resonate with us in ways that statistics and numbers can't because they provide an emotional connection to the audience.

Stories increase value, as seen in the Significant Objects Project, which proved that attaching a back story to simple everyday items made them more valuable in the eyes of the audience.

Try following the Pixar formula by making your team the hero of your story and then take that to the next level by making the customer the hero of your team's story.

Storytelling platforms can increase ROI over time and are much more effective than any one-time, value-based event.

Chapter 8:
SELL THE STORY

For employees who aren't the top leader at a company, it can be difficult to get ideas through the bureaucratic machine. We've got the idea, we've got the knowledge to implement the idea, and we've got the data to back up its success. All we need is the go-ahead and the resources from our boss. We know our idea would manage incredible gains, but our boss may not take the time to hear it out or even consider what we're proposing. What next? Do we let it go? That is often the path of least resistance.

That ends now. Bosses who won't champion employee ideas can be convinced! We have to believe and trust in this proven process. In some cases, bad bosses are the best place to start implementing a culture of empathy. They've got to get on board anyway if we have any hope of persuading the rest of the company to follow suit. What can we do? How can we sell our bosses on the idea of empathy, or on any idea?

Rena Patel is living proof of how well pushing back can work. Rena is the former digital advertising and brand campaign manager at consulting services company Capgemini and now serves as the Chief Marketing Officer of the consulting division for research and consulting firm Kantar. At Capgemini, Rena had two goals. The first was to increase revenue growth for their IT services. The second was to increase the overall awareness of the brand and also the reputation of the consultants they worked with, their experts.

Up to that point, Rena was handling many tasks—tweets, campaigns, press releases, and talking up the company on all the latest marketing channels. Capgemini competes with well-known brands like KPMG, Deloitte, and Accenture, but they felt that they were falling behind their competitors.

When the executives looked at the company's competitors, they noticed that they all sponsored ads in airports, golf tournaments, and even professional golfers. They also spent large amounts of money on more traditional advertising that was very hard to measure. Rena had tried some of these methods and demonstrated that they weren't working. They were expensive and hard to track. She believed there had to be a better way.

When the executives saw their competition running ads in golf magazines and airports, sponsoring golfers and golf tournaments, what do you think the executive team asked Rena to do—sponsor a golfer. The CMO was likely excited about the idea as well because that would mean getting a huge sponsorship budget; the cost of sponsoring well-known athletes is easily in the millions of dollars. Rena's colleagues even started talking about how awesome it would be to have front-row seats at the golf tournaments and to meet the famous golfers.

But instead of jumping on board with the plan, Rena pushed back. Instead of following the org chart, the traditional organizational model, she decided to ask the question: what's in it for the customer?

Rena looked at the content the company created, and she learned that they were far behind their competitors. They simply didn't produce content that engaged their audience. She relayed this to the executives and said she felt it was the reason why they didn't have a greater awareness in the global consulting services market.

Rena was trying to put the customer at the center of the org chart, so she rephrased the question more directly to incorporate what her bosses wanted: what's in it for the customer to sponsor a golfer?

She didn't just pose the question, she set out to answer that question. She did so by asking her customers. She spoke to her customers and found out that most of them were not golfers. She found out that most of them didn't like golf. They didn't watch golf tournaments. They didn't even know the names of many of the famous golfers except maybe Tiger Woods.

That got Rena thinking. With a significantly lower budget, she felt she could create content that delivered on the value by reaching, engaging, even converting the buyers they weren't already reaching by creating content that their customers actually wanted. Rena believed that this effort would deliver sales growth, increase their awareness, and help to build the reputation of their consultants.

Rena told her boss that with a small percent of the cost of a golf sponsorship, she believed she could raise awareness, build the reputation of their consultants, and bring nearly a million new visitors to their website, all very ambitious goals. She was even bold enough to say that her boss could hold her accountable if the project failed.

With the support of both the executives and her team, Rena created a brand storytelling site called Content-Loop.com. She set out to answer the real questions on the minds of their buyers. She started tracking the engagement the company received when they published content about topics like Big Data, Cloud, Technology, and all the subjects of Capgemini consulting projects.

And as promised, at the end of one year, Rena had delivered nearly one million new visitors to their website. They saw more than 100,000 new followers to their company page on LinkedIn and were adding 3,000 to 4,000 additional new followers per week. They had 1.8 million shares across LinkedIn in that first year as well. Better yet, Rena told me that the program generated nearly one million dollars in sales in that first year. We can imagine how happy our bosses would be if we were responsible for bringing in an additional one million dollars in sales for our company, maybe even so happy that they give us a raise or promotion.

What's so fascinating about Rena's story is that even after delivering those staggering results for such a small percent of the budget of sponsoring a pro golfer, the executives there still wanted to sponsor a golfer. I imagine that executives of a company that can afford to sponsor famous golfers would be quite proud of their company when they see their company logo on a pro athlete's hat or shirt. I can understand the tug on the ego. But Rena didn't give in. She pushed back again by coming back with another proposition.

During her quest to publish content that her customers wanted, Rena learned that a large portion of her audience found the company's content on LinkedIn. They read articles and went back to connect with the authors of those articles. Some of those proposals converted to sales.

Rena went back to her boss and asked for twice her previous budget (still only a small percent of what it would cost for a golf sponsorship). She believed that this would allow her to deliver double the brand awareness and possibly even double the sales. Did she achieve her goal and show her team the value of putting customers ahead of executive egos?

In the second year of the program, Rena was able to contribute nearly five million dollars in revenue. She told me that the program worked because it integrated the human element of the company—focusing on turning employees into brand advocates. By the third year, there were over 1,000 employees creating and sharing business-related content across social channels.

Rena left the company shortly after that to join LinkedIn because she wanted to share her success with other brands. She then became the global head of brand and communications and now is the CMO, Consulting, at Kantar. All of this happened because Rena pushed back against the organizational pressure from above and remained focused on what was in it for the customer while tapping into her employee expertise to deliver ROI. It also happened because the executives at Capgemini championed Rena's ideas. They allowed her to push back. They put faith in Rena because they believed that she showed empathy for their business goals and because she convinced them of the value of using empathy for customers to achieve those business goals.

Three years ago, I was presenting this amazing story of Rena's push back and her million-dollar sales wins to a technology company's marketing leaders. At the end of the presentation, one of the attendees shared that he had just left Capgemini. It turned out that it was his job to manage the developers who built the platform. He told me that the platform Rena built was contributing more than twenty million dollars per year, making this one of the most successful marketing programs I have ever heard about.

SELLING YOUR BOSS ON THE IDEA OF EMPATHY

We've talked about numerous ways to grow a culture of empathy from the standpoint of the customer and the employee but that still leaves the boss out of the equation. How do you explain the importance of empathy to executives who don't have any? That's a joke, but there is no question that empathy is in short supply in most organizations.

The answer is simple. Take some advice from the movie *Jerry Maguire* and show them the money! In many businesses, bottom line driven executives aren't persuaded by the idea of empathy as a means to increase revenue after the first pitch. Naturally, profitability and revenue drive most bosses to encourage certain ideas at work. Or it is their egos that make them think they know better?

Effective leaders are tuned into the fact that the company needs to, of course, make enough money to be profitable. Because of that, some managers aren't inclined to dump resources into projects aimed with fluffier goals, like creating a more cohesive workplace culture. Too many managers and leaders are skeptical about using empathy as a true business asset because its business contributions might seem abstract. To the managers who value profit over employee well-being, people can seem somewhat disposable: Their thinking is that they can always hire new employees. Those kinds of managers miss the fact that empathy bolsters employee engagement and retention, and it actually does increase revenue.

The idea of empathy as a business asset remains a tough sell. But not to worry: We can take concrete steps to change our boss' mindset toward the issues with our culture in the workplace.

Change begins with the people surrounding those managers. Bad bosses who treat employees like followers often have unhappy teams working below them. Much of the time, the managers aren't getting much feedback from the people they manage—if any at all—that will lead them to reflect on their leadership style or change the way they approach their roles as managers.

They've been promoted or hired into these leadership positions and often bad managers believe it is exactly their worst traits that have made them successful. That is why empathy is so counterintuitive. We believe that in order to be successful in life, we need to act mean. (Nice guys and gals finish last, right?)

In a traditional company hierarchy, even if some managers buy into a culture of empathy for their teams, their peers aren't going to be much help. In a hierarchy where managers prioritize getting to the top of the food chain over anything else, leaders rarely give each other advice for better management styles. Why bother when we know it'll just be shut down?

But if we never challenge our leaders' ways of doing things, we'll just continue to hate our jobs until we decide to leave our companies. And then we'll find new jobs and new managers to hate. If we want to find truly fulfilling work lives, we've got to break that cycle at some point.

You can make a big impact on the culture that permeates your workplace, starting with the person directly above you in the hierarchy. The key to persuading your boss is to approach selling the idea of empathy at the right time when they've just knocked down another one of your ideas. To convince your boss that a culture of empathy can also help accomplish the same goals you are aiming to achieve, you've got to speak your boss' language.

HOW THE PUSH BACK WORKS

The push back challenges managers to think outside their comfort zones and simply challenging our bosses' bad ideas creates a more efficient company culture. This then creates stronger connections between teams in an organization because it encourages employees to ask the tough questions and solidifies the notion that team members are giving their honest input. It will also disrupt the dreaded Illusion Point (Chapter 1), challenge the leader, and question status quo ideas that get in our way and keep us from accomplishing our team's ambitious goals. It puts the onus on our managers to explain why our ideas aren't being taken more seriously when we know they're valuable ones. When we approach our push back in a strategic way, our bosses will buy into the success we've shown them.

Unfortunately, there is no way around this step. It's essential that your manager is involved in creating a culture of empathy at your company. Leaders have to lead by example. Otherwise, changes won't be made by any other employees because all of us need to feel that our leaders are in it with us and that they won't be punished for pursuing new ideas.

STEP #1: Examine the way we've presented our ideas in the past.

Have we convincingly presented our ideas or have we just assumed our manager won't go for it? When you feel that Illusion Point starting to approach, do you go along with your boss' ideas or do you challenge them?

More than likely you've accepted that your manager doesn't care about your input and you've done the tasks he or she asks of you.

That may have helped you stay in his or her good graces but it's probably also led to unfulfilling work.

Obviously, you don't want to risk your reputation within your company by stepping too far out of line when you push for your ideas. That fine line can be difficult to gauge but think about what your boss' overarching goals have been in the past. How do we strategically challenge our boss without coming across as too pushy or unprofessional?

STEP #2: Ask the right questions.

The thought of challenging your boss in any way is daunting, but there's an easy formula for approaching challenging managers and getting the most out of your meetings with them.

You want to prioritize your ideas in the moment, while also challenging your boss to think critically about why they're not receptive to your ideas. Once you recognize the Illusion Point— when your manager suggests counterproductive, status quo ideas to accomplish a goal—push back by asking three simple questions to stop a bad idea right in its tracks.

Question #1: *Why does this matter?*

The strategies we implement at work take time and energy— your time and energy, and your colleagues' time and energy. Sure, there are yes men and women in your company, but that doesn't bring any meaning into the work that gets done. Being a yes man or woman doesn't make you a better employee. Traditional company structures might reward those employees at times, but in the end, it just makes you an average employee.

Let's be real. If you're going to dedicate so much of your time to a project at work, you want it to be worthwhile. Asking why any strategy or new tactic matters will show you care about what your work means once it's out in the world. Your manager should be able to explain how something you'll be tasked with supports the mission and goals of your team. If he or she is unable to do that, there's something flawed in the plan.

A leader should be able to explain why an idea matters to the company but also to customers. Making sure an idea matters to the right people is critical. Are we sure it's going to resonate with our audience? What audience are we trying to resonate with anyway? Knowing who you're talking to—and who you should be talking to—saves a lot of money. Spending time on a project that may not be what an audience is looking for would waste resources that could be spent somewhere else.

Discussing why implementing a new idea matters also gets the conversation started, and your boss may be forced to explain the thinking behind it better. That opens the door for more conversation and perhaps a better understanding between your two schools of thought. From the boss' standpoint, that helps build a culture of empathy, too. Being in the know keeps employees more satisfied and keeps managers on their toes. When employees ask why an idea matters, it helps bosses be better bosses.

A good answer to that question should yield insight that everyone would jump on board with. An example of a good answer is "we understand our customers are changing and we need to change with them."

What's a bad answer?

"Because I said so."

"Because our VP said it's important."

"Because this is just the way it's done here."

Those kinds of answers deserve a push back.

Question #2: *What's the impact?*

Questioning your manager on the impact of the tasks he or she has assigned you is a good way to ensure you're keeping the customer in focus. It shows you're aware and tuned in to how new ideas may change the customer experience. It shows that, even if your manager is excited about an idea, it's still an issue if it won't work for the customer. This question brings the customer back into the conversation.

Asking about an idea's impact also makes it clear you know what's expected of you as you execute that idea. It shows how important it is for you and your boss. If you're expected to deliver certain results for your customer, you should have a good handle on what those results look like. If there's a disconnect between what your manager wants and how you think the customer might react, this is the question to get that conversation started. How will this project impact your customer's experience? Your workload? Will this idea take away from your loyal customers to chase a new audience? All are good questions, and all are worth asking.

The impact of any idea or project is something that should be hashed out before it's executed. Once the idea is in motion, it could be too late to counter negative consequences. While we want to incorporate some risk into our business, keeping the impact on the customer at the front of your mind during the discussion stage will ensure you have the best outcome possible. More importantly, there won't be any surprises when it comes time to measure the results.

Question #3: *How will this be measured?*

Everyone wants to be good at his or her job, and our managers want us to be good at them, too. But being good at our jobs requires a certain level of clarity. For bosses who don't usually discuss the meaning or impact behind an idea they've proposed, the milestones they want us to accomplish probably aren't all that clear, either. That means the intended result can be something of a gray area.

To accomplish that bigger goal, we need to solidify the milestones in the middle. Knowing the details of what your manager expects when you're executing that idea in real time matters. The end goal might be admirable, but what good is executing an idea well without a measuring system to track that success?

As with the other two questions, this one provides an avenue for the all-important dialogue between you and your bosses, which is what these questions are all about. "When you say you want to see a bigger audience tapped into our marketing content, what exactly does that mean?" "How are we going to actually measure those terms?" "Without incorporating a measurement system into your plan, it's nearly impossible to discuss your project's success in concrete terms."

On a positive note, measuring the outcomes specifically also helps to ensure the idea is repeated efficiently and correctly if it works well. Measuring also helps us to understand what went wrong if the work doesn't go as we'd hoped. With parameters, we can mark off where we fell short, as opposed to making guesses. They will also prevent us from making the same mistake twice. Ensuring that everyone's expectations are laid out concretely keeps everyone's goals aligned.

If your boss' idea is a flop, measuring its success in an agreed-up-on fashion will help illustrate that for future projects. Even if your boss isn't willing to admit the ideas he or she has brought to the table in the past haven't been any good, measuring ideas will force him to come to terms with that in the future. In a boss' world, presenting clear, measured results is the best way to grab attention. Once you've developed a measurement system, there's no denying a project's level of success or failure.

Why does this matter? What's the impact? How will it be measured? These three questions are simple and logical. They help to start a dialogue with your manager while also showing you care about your work.

USE EMPATHY TO SELL EMPATHY

Selling the idea of empathy to our managers requires a dose or two of empathy as well. We often try to sell our main points in all the wrong ways. We discuss numbers and relevant data. We show examples from other companies that experienced success using similar tactics and throw out all kinds of boring statistics. We want to come off as reasonable and measured, which is understandable. While research to support every good idea is important, you need your boss' attention.

Do you remember the example we discussed earlier regarding Save the Children? Their storytelling campaign had generated more donations than the campaigns that had centered around facts and figures. Executives may not understand empathy or the importance of it, but that doesn't mean that they can't be swayed by it themselves. They may be laser-focused on ROI but they are still human. Reason and data won't stick in their brains the way a story with an emotional appeal does.

We can put it all together and utilize the tools we've been discussing. We can couple your facts and figures with storytelling and emotional appeal. We can take a more narrative approach and work on finding anecdotal evidence to bolster your research. We can tell a story that demonstrates how your ideas can increase revenue.

WHAT YOU NEED TO KNOW!

Don't give up on a great idea just because you don't get immediate approval from your boss.

Learn to speak your boss' language and show them the money!

Utilize the push back. Ask the important questions. Why does this matter? What's the impact? How will this be measured?

Use empathy to sell empathy. Don't rely on dry facts and figures. Persuade your boss through storytelling.

Chapter 9:
BE KIND. BE COOL. BE YOU.

A culture of empathy doesn't only benefit the company, it brings employees closer with each other while building morale and trust. When you treat others with empathy, your coworkers will have your back.

Remember the story of how I was fired? Surprisingly enough, my time with that company didn't end there. Just two weeks later, the chairman of the company's board called me unexpectedly and said they wanted to hire me back.

It wasn't my direct boss who had a change of heart. It was the sales team, and a few of the more outspoken individuals, who persuaded him that he had made a major mistake. I will forever be grateful to those people (Libby, Mellissa, and Greg, to name a few of them) who fought for me at that time.

They all believed the marketing plan I put together was exactly what they needed to get the company back in shape. When I got the call from the chairman, who told me that he had fired the person who had fired me, and learned they wanted me to return to the company, I was shocked. But that's what I did.

Honestly, I didn't really have a choice. My wife and I were crashing with my in-laws, and I wanted to implement the plan I had put together and start seeing results. And it worked! In less than a year, traffic to their website doubled and leads for the sales team tripled.

I didn't realize it at the time, but there was a silver lining to that whole experience. It was in the network of connections I had made throughout the company because I had worked to have real empathy for my colleagues, my peers, and our customers. They showed me what the real problems were. They helped me figure out what kind of plan we needed. And they fought for me when I needed them most. I will never forget that. They also made me realize all the great managers I had before (Liz, Kerry, Dave, Laurie, Danny, Bob, Jim, Lori, Michele, Greg, Susan) and they also made me realize that sometimes we learn the most from those who challenge us.

Genuine empathy creates loyalty and dependability. Dependability is crucial for fostering trust among coworkers, spouses, friends—it's the glue that holds us together and keeps our life and our work environments less chaotic. When employees know they can rely on one another, they will want to collaborate; they won't fear being forced to work together.

DON'T BE THE ONE WHO SUCKS!

Let's say that you meet two people for the first time. The first person talks about him or herself constantly, but the second person asks you questions.

You are more likely to gravitate toward that second person because that person is showing empathy for you. That person is taking an interest in you. It's true on the bigger scale with how companies approach their customers, and it's also true for personal interactions. Whether you're a manager, employee, spouse, parent, or friend, simply asking other people questions and taking an interest in them and their concerns, will cause them to like you more.

Following are five simple ways that you can begin utilizing empathy today to improve your life at work or at home, so you don't suck, and you aren't the person everyone else around you complains about to others.

1. Learn to listen.

Asking questions is crucial, but it's only half the battle. You need to listen to the answers.

This is easier said than done. We're all distracted by what's going on around us—our phone buzzing, the 129 emails in our inbox, our friend's updates on Facebook or Snapchat. We have so many opportunities to look away when someone is talking.

Listening does not mean thinking about how you're going to respond to what someone is saying. Truly listening requires putting your own agenda aside and trying to understand where the other person is coming from.

Listening is not an entirely selfless act. If you stop and take the time to listen, you will be surprised by what you learn. Look at how much damage managers who don't listen can cause, or spouses who have grown tired of their partners' concerns.

We don't need to make that same mistake. We should leave ourselves open to constructive criticism and feedback. Not every idea is worth taking, but we won't have the chance if we don't listen.

2. Try being kind.

Empathy is so much more than being nice and kind, but nowhere does it say that you can't be kind. In fact, kindness seems to be in short supply. Our lives and workplaces have become especially toxic. How many times have you witnessed or experienced inappropriate behavior at work? How often does it occur? If you haven't, consider yourself lucky, but by no means is it the norm. At times, it feels like the workplace is the last place you might find kindness.

"Kindness is contagious" is the phrase used by Stanford psychologist Jamil Zaki, who conducted a study that reinforced his theory of "positive conformity." His theory claims that those who believe others are generous would then act more generous themselves.

This isn't a new philosophy. It's been said countless different ways. You've heard the phrase, "you catch more flies with honey than with vinegar"? The concept is simple, and it's one you've most likely experienced. It's easier to get what you want from others when you're nice. Reverse the roles. Would you be more likely to help a friend who is bitter and jaded or someone generous and trusting?

It all goes back to the golden rule: Treat others as you would like to be treated. It doesn't take much effort at all. We may be surprised by how far a simple "good morning" and a sincere "how are you?" can take us.

3. Don't take it personally.

These days, it's not uncommon to see tweets and stories go viral about bad airline experiences that call out certain airlines for poor customer service or about a negative overall customer experience.

This topic came up during a dinner conversation I recently had with my good friends Ann Handley and John Hall. I told my colleagues that I tend not to complain about airlines, despite how much I travel and how often I've experienced the delays that keep me from my family and the lost bags.

The reason I don't complain is that often flight delays are caused by the weather. I can't blame someone for the weather. And I have found, that in most cases, if you look at the nature of the complaints most people have with airlines, they tend to be about individual experiences that a customer had with an employee who might just be having a bad day. The way I see it, American Airlines is just as likely to have an employee having a bad day as an employee at United Airlines.

How many times have you had a bad day and later felt guilty for how you handled a personal interaction? It happens to you, and it happens to others, so the next time you have a frustrating experience with a boss, coworker, friend, or family member, try taking the empathetic approach. Put yourself in the other person's shoes. Don't take it personally and consider that the other person might be having a bad day.

Dr. Emiliana Simon-Thomas teaches a course at University of California, Berkeley called The Science of Happiness and cites how people respond to adversity as one of the key habits that determine their happiness at work[xxxvii]. If you make a mistake or get yelled at by your boss, you could become defensive and avoid putting yourself out there during future projects, or you could think of the experience as temporary and work to be better next time.

She teaches us that with every setback and obstacle, you have the choice to go backward or to go forward. Your choice will go far in dictating your effectiveness as an employee and, in the long run, your overall happiness.

4. Remember the good times.

I did not love many of my 53 jobs. If you're anything like me, I bet there are jobs in your past that you hated as well. Maybe you even hate your current job. That's not uncommon, but it's important to realize that it's not all negative.

We spend so much of our time at work that, even if we hate our jobs, we are bound to share laughs and experience our share of memorable moments with other employees. That's true of every one of the jobs I've hated. The position itself may have been less than desirable and not a good fit but that didn't stop me from enjoying moments. I've made friends at every job I've had, and I've learned the most from the mean people I worked for or with.

It's so easy to get caught up in the negative, but when shifting your focus from dwelling on the negative to appreciating the positive, it changes your mindset. It leaves you more open to positive experiences. And sometimes, it just makes you feel better. Things are rarely as bad as they seem.

5. Find meaning in what we do.

Or more simply, Be kind. Be cool. Be you.

THE SECRET TO A HAPPY & MEANINGFUL LIFE

We all want to feel invested in a larger purpose—to enjoy our jobs, create value, and make an impact. If you can't find that larger purpose in the work itself, you might find it in working together with your teammates or colleagues.

Meaning within a company is also part of what attracts customers to our brands in the first place. Customers can sense when a company's employees are passionate about their work or when employees are simply going through the motions. Meaning is also important for the success of future teams. If employees are unhappy because they don't feel a sense of purpose, they're less likely to encourage other employees to go the extra mile.

We all want what we do for eight hours a day to matter to the world. We want to know we're having an impact in the grand scheme of things. Without that feeling, we tend to get apathetic about our goals. Multiple studies and dozens of books have discussed the primary role that purpose plays in our overall job satisfaction. That's true even in jobs we don't particularly enjoy.

Purpose doesn't have to always depend on our passion. No job is perfect in every way; there's always going to be some level of drudgery. To find meaning, sometimes we just need to adjust our mindsets away from the tedious, frustrating work we do to find the deeper purpose of the daily grind. What kind of person do you want to be? What's the bigger goal? If you can see through the monotony in pursuit of a bigger goal, your work will seem much more meaningful, even if at the moment it's not what you want to be doing.

"What's the secret to your success?"

Someone asked me that once and, totally flattered, I really had to think before answering. If you had asked me in college what I wanted to do with my life, I certainly wouldn't have said I wanted to grow up to be a marketing consultant. I've had so many ups and downs, and much of my success I attribute to luck. *How did*

I even get to where I am?

When I got out of college, I did what many of us do. I took the first job that came along. Young and broke, we often have student loans to pay, apartments to find, and lives to live, so many of us find a job that the world seems to have told us it wants us to take. Maybe we lean toward a certain line of work because of our passions, serendipity, or just plain luck (good and bad!). Either way, that first job allows us to get paid, pay the bills, and start on something we can call a career path. If it's relevant to our major, great! If not, we'll just figure out that part later.

Life is good for a while. We're living independently and working a "real job." Then we learn job skills. We develop expertise and networks in our field that prime us for more responsibility in that industry. When they need certain positions filled by people with a particular skill set, we're able to fill the role. In other words, we develop a career path by pursuing what we know. We settle on a job we trained for or that was an extension of our first job. "I studied accounting, so I became an accountant. Now I'm a partner at an accounting firm." That is a common scenario. Maybe you know someone like that. Maybe it's you!

Many of us find ourselves in jobs like this because we asked our college counselor *what the world needs.* He or she said that accounting firms are always hiring, so we studied accounting and became an accountant. Now you're getting paid to do a job the world needs, and over time you've become an expert. But is it enough?

One day, we look around and realize that we've been spending our days (or years) working a job we didn't really want. Or, we just get bored. That accountant realizes he's not doing what he was born to do. It's not his or her passion. That gets us to start thinking about the job that we really want. *What was I born to do? What do I love?* These questions are not easy to answer because sometimes the thing we are good at isn't the thing we were born to choose as our life's passion.

The opposite is true as well. I love the band the Foo Fighters. I know every song they've ever written. I'm a huge fan of their founder and lead singer, Dave Grohl, and know about how he survived the death of his friend Kurt Cobain, swore off hard drugs, talks about his love for his kids and wife in interviews, and taught himself how to play the drums. And every time I talk about the band, my wife looks at me like I need to rethink my life. I love their music, and I know all about them. I would like to be just like them, but the world doesn't need me singing Foo Fighter songs.

Once, I was giving a keynote presentation on the power of connecting with what your customers want and, of course, I was going on and on about Dave Grohl and the Foo Fighters. Afterward, I checked for any tweets of my speech and found that someone had shared this picture:

[H/T: UPROXX, photo via Reddit]

The lesson: We can try and learn the things that we might love to do. And we can all hope to be recognized as a success in that pursuit of a passion. But those who have found happiness in their life and their work are often working in the service of others.

Dave Grohl writes and sings songs; he plays the guitar and the drums and performs for millions of raving fans. But he seems to care about people not just in the work he does, he goes the extra step. He pours his fans a beer when their cups run low. He focuses on what his customers want and need.

I was speaking at an international conference with my fellow speaker and author friend, Carla Johnson, when she introduced me to a brilliant professor of Design Thinking from the United Arab Emirates University, Jose Berengueres. In the conversation, I mentioned my book and explained the key concepts. Then, he asked me if I had ever heard of the Japanese term ikigai. I had not, so I looked it up.

Longevity researcher and author Dan Buettner heard this term used by the people in Okinawa, Japan. The city was in what he called a "blue zone," a place where people often live to 100 years with relative health and vigor into their old age. In Japanese, the term translates roughly into "reason for being," but those in Okinawa would translate it to mean "reason to get out of bed" or even "reason for living."

This image shows how I see what ikigai means. I think it's really a formula for happiness in business and life. It's similar to the kind of questions that career coaches might ask. But the visual really sticks with me, and I hope it helps you to see the path you might take to find happiness and success in your own career. Your reason for being is likely a unique combination and intersection of four factors.

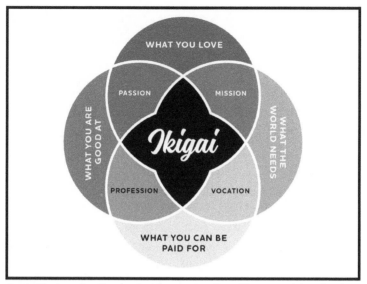

Inspired by: https://medium.com/social-enterprise-alliance/the-secrets-of-ikigai-b39cb-fa693b5

We all have something that we would love to do with our lives, but if the world doesn't need it, we would be happy but poor. If we do what we love, but we don't know what we're doing, that's a pipedream. The other side of the coin is finding a job that we know, but don't love, and we sacrifice our happiness. So, what is the best path to take? Start by asking yourself four important questions:

1. What do I know?

2. What does the world need?

3. What do I love?

4. What are people willing to pay me to do?

I call the intersection of these four elements "The Secret of Life" or "The Secret to a Happy Life." We all want to feel competent in our jobs, as a bare minimum. We need to do something the world needs or we wouldn't get hired to do it. We all want to love what we do, though we usually see that as a bonus. And finally, we all want to be recognized as a leader in our field.

All of us must find a balance between purpose and profit. So, let's take the essence of those four questions and boil it down to one question that you can ask yourself:

What need in the world inspires my passion, and how can I apply my unique expertise or experience to serve that need and get paid in the process?

That is the secret to happiness and success if we want to live a life of meaning. It's true about people, and it's also true about companies. Try posing those same questions you just asked yourself about your company.

1. What do we know and what's our expertise?

2. What does the world truly want or need?

3. What is our passion as an organization and what is it that we love?

4. How does that intersect with what the world truly values?

Answer these questions. Then, make a plan to move closer to your best life.

BEFORE YOU GO

We all want the same things, don't we? We want to love our jobs, to feel fulfilled by our careers.

We want to make a difference, to do great things with our "one wild and precious life," as the poet Mary Oliver wrote.

Yet most of us are not happy. We aren't fulfilled. Fighting on Facebook is almost a national pastime.

We are experiencing a crisis of empathy and engagement. Mean people suck! But what can we do?

Here's my advice: make a choice.

Make a choice to not be unhappy, unfulfilled, disengaged and focus on others. Apply empathy where it matters the most. Make a choice for empathy—in business, in life.

With empathy, you can find the meaning in the connections all around you. With empathy, you can understand the purpose in your career. With empathy, you can find a way to enjoy your job, create real meaning for your customers and fellow employees, and make a difference both in your work and within your organization.

Here's the truth: Each of us is born with the capacity for deep empathy. As we grow, we learn that we have to defend ourselves. And slowly over time, some of that capacity for empathy is diminished and replaced by our belief that we have to take what we want.

But ironically, empathy can get you what you need. Showing others that you care is the best way to get what you want (and to live a better life in the process).

Empathy is the secret to success in business and life. Now more than ever, we need it. And we need to remind ourselves to reflect on it every day.

And now, it's your turn. It's up to you. So, before you go…one more question remains.

The question is: what choice will you make?

WHAT YOU NEED TO KNOW!

When you treat others with empathy, they will treat you with empathy in return. This has a positive impact on everyone around you and can also help you make strong connections. Who will have your back when things get tough?

Don't forget the golden rule: treat others the way you want to be treated.

Find the balance between what you know, what you love, what the world needs, and what has real value.

Focus and nurture your empathy for others every day.

THE END

ENDNOTE BIBLIOGRAPHY

i. Harter, Jim. "Employee Engagement on the Rise in the U.S." Gallup. August 26, 2018. https://news.gallup.com/poll/241649/employee-engagement-rise.aspx

ii. Collie, Leah. "Toddler can't help but tear up while watching a dinosaur fall down." Mashable. September 21, 2017. https://mashable.com/2017/09/21/toddler-crying-pixar-movie/

iii. Knapton, Sarah. "Empathetic people are made, not born, new research suggests." The Telegraph. March 12, 2018. https://www.telegraph.co.uk/science/2018/03/12/empathetic-people-made-not-born-new-research-suggests/

iv. Riess, M.D., Helen. "The Science of Empathy." *Journal of Patient Experience.* May 9, 2017. https://www.ncbi.nlm.nih.gov/pmc/articles/PMC5513638/#bibr1-2374373517699267

v. O'Brien, Keith. "The empathy deficit." Boston.com. October 17, 2010. archive.boston.com/bostonglobe/ideas/articles/2010/10/17/the_empathy_deficit/

vi. Whitby, Bob. "Empathy and Perception of Others Shapes Political Ideology, Study Finds." University of Arkansas. April 9, 2019. https://news.uark.edu/articles/47824/empathy-and-perception-of-others-shapes-political-ideology-study-finds

vii. Executive Summary. "2018 State of Workplace Empathy." Businessolver. 2018. https://info.businessolver.com/empathy-2018-executive-summary

viii. Kopec, Marisa. "It's Not Content—It's a Lack of Buyer Insights That's the Problem." SiriusDecisions. January 29, 2014. https://www.siriusdecisions.com/blog/its-not-content--its-a-lack-of-buyer-insights-thats-the-problem

ix. Upland Kapost. "Marketing's $958 Million Problem: Quantifying the Cost of Inefficient Content Processes." Accessed June 18, 2019. http://resources.kapost.com/the-cost-of-marketing-inefficiency.html

x. Integration Training. "The Real Org Chart." Accessed June 18, 2019. https://www.integrationtraining.co.uk/

xi. Baer, Jay. *Hug Your Haters.* Accessed June 18, 2019. https://www.jaybaer.com/hug-your-haters/

xii. The Wharton School. "Microsoft CEO Satya Nadella: How Empathy Sparks Innovation." February 22, 2018. https://knowledge.wharton.upenn.edu/article/microsofts-ceo-on-how-empathy-sparks-innovation/

xiii. Most Over and Under-Rated CEOs http://fortune.com/2019/01/22/most-over-and-underrated-ceos/

xiv. Naughton, John. "Could Kodak's demise have been averted?" The Guardian. January 21, 2012. https://www.theguardian.com/technology/2012/jan/22/john-naughton-kodak-lessons

xv. Ng, Desmond. "How a rookie brought Lego back from the brink." CNA. January 30, 2017. https://www.channelnewsasia.com/news/cnainsider/how-a-rookie-brought-lego-back-from-the-brink-7550676

xvi. Davis, Johnny. "How Lego clicked: the super brand that reinvented itself." The Guardian. June 4, 2017. https://www.theguardian.com/lifeandstyle/2017/jun/04/how-lego-clicked-the-super-brand-that-reinvented-itself

xvii. Haden, Jeff. "This Study of 400,000 People Reveals the 1 Reason Employees Work Harder (and It's Not Pay or Benefits or Culture Decks)." Inc. January 4, 2018. https://www.inc.com/jeff-haden/this-study-of-400000-people-reveals-1-reason-employees-work-harder-and-its-not-pay-or-benefits-or-culture-decks.html

xviii. Lebowitz, Shana. "Google considers this to be the most critical trait of successful teams." *Business Insider.* November 20, 2015. https://www.businessinsider.com/amy-edmondson-on-psychological-safety-2015-11

xix. Neisser, Drew. "How to Grow Marketing Innovation In-House" AdAge. May 18, 2016. https://adage.com/article/cmo-strategy/grow-innovation-house/304050

xx. Wong, Kristin. "What Employees Value More Than Salary, According to Glassdoor." Lifehacker. January 17, 2017. https://twocents.lifehacker.com/what-employees-value-more-than-salary-according-to-gla-1791184497

xxi. Barsh, Joanna, Marla M. Capozzi, and Jonathan Davidson. "Leadership and innovation." McKinsey & Company. January 2008. https://www.mckinsey.com/business-functions/strategy-and-corporate-finance/our-insights/leadership-and-innovation

xxii. DiSalvo, David. "10 Reasons Why We Struggle With Creativity." *Psychology Today.* March 26, 2013. https://www.psychologytoday.com/us/blog/neuronarrative/201303/10-reasons-why-we-struggle-creativity

xxiii. The Economist: Business. "A hard act to follow." The Economist. June 27, 2014. https://www.economist.com/business/2014/06/27/a-hard-act-to-follow

xxiv. Durden, Tyler. "The Fortune 500's Fastest Growing (And Shrinking) Companies. ZeroHedge. April 5, 2017. https://www.zerohedge.com/news/2017-04-05/fortune-500s-fastest-growing-and-shrinking-companies

xxv. LinkedIn SlideShare. "The Buyer Journey Has Changed." November 18, 2013. https://www.slideshare.net/BizoInc/2013-dreamforce-breakout/3-The_Buyers_Journey_Has_ChangedThe

xxvi. Neff, Jack. "P&G Has Best Quarter In 5 Years Despite Marketing Cuts." AdAge. October 19, 2018. https://adage.com/article/cmo-strategy/p-g-quarter-years-cutting-marketing/315334

xxvii. Neff, Jack. "Are Brands Optimizing Their Marketing to Death?" AdAge. August 22, 2016. https://adage.com/article/print-edition/killing-brands-soft-ly-optimizing/305543

xxviii. Fenn, Noah. "Despite All This Data, Empathy Is Still the Greatest Tool in a Marketer's Toolbox." AdAge. April 22, 2016. https://adage.com/article/digitalnext/empathy-greatest-tool-a-marketer-s-toolbox/303674

xxvix. Schultz, E.J. "Coke Global CMO To Depart Amid Leadership Changes." AdAge. March 23, 2017. https://adage.com/article/cmo-strategy/coke-global-cmo-depart-amid-leadership/308403

xxx. Havas Group, Vivendi. Meaningful Brands video, 2:40. Accessed June 20, 2019. http://www.meaningful-brands.com/en

xxxi. Fast Company Brandless Company Page. "Most Innovative Companies: Brandless." Fast Company. Accessed June 20, 2019. https://www.fastcompany.com/company/brandless

xxxii. Castelloe, M. (2016, December 23). The Evolutionary Origins of Empathy. Retrieved from https://www.psychologytoday.com/us/blog/the-me-in-we/201612/the-evolutionary-origins-empathy

xxxiii. Boris, Vanessa. "What Makes Storytelling So Effective For Learning." *Harvard Business Publishing.* December 20, 2017. https://www.harvardbusiness.org/what-makes-storytelling-so-effective-for-learning/

xxxiv. Miller, Michele. "The Art of Effective Storytelling." LinkedIn SlideShare. May 19, 2015. https://www.slideshare.net/michelelanemiller/the-art-of-48353000

xxxv. Duhigg, Charles. "How the Disney Hit 'Frozen' Was Almost a Massive Failure." *Reader's Digest.* Excerpt from Smarter Faster Better, Penguin Random House, 2016. https://www.rd.com/advice/work-career/frozen-movie-almost-failure/

xxxvi. ANA.net (Login required.) "Taking Marketing To New Heights." October 25, 2016. https://www.ana.net/magazines/show/id/41836

xxxvii. Humphrey, Judith. "The Science Of Happiness." Fast Company. April 6, 2018. https://www.fastcompany.com/40554865/the-science-of-happiness-in-four-simple-work-habits